HIGH-PROOF PDX

A SPIRITED GUIDE
to
PORTLAND'S
CRAFT DISTILLING
SCENE

by
KAREN LOCKE

Overcup Press
2017

First Overcup Press printing, September 2017

Illustrations by Ilan Schraer
Book Design by Carla Girard

ISBN: 978-0983491767

Printed in China

Library of Congress Cataloging-in Publication data is on file with publisher.

highproofpdx.com
overcupbooks.com

Overcup Press
4207 SE Woodstock Blvd #253
Portland, OR 97206

This is for you, Portland.

CONTENTS

HIGH-PROOF PDX

PDX

A Spirited Guide
to
Portland's Craft Distilling Scene

by
KAREN LOCKE

A Letter to the Drinker

Dear Portland Drinker,

Blue Curaçao and half-and-half. These are two of the main ingredients in a cocktail made in a Minneapolis Thai bar and restaurant where I worked as a server in my early twenties. Sadly, it had been on the cocktail menu since the 1990s, without so much as an update, occasionally getting some curious diner's attention.

When customers would ask me about this outlandishly blue and creamy drink, I'd try my best to dissuade them from ordering it. Then one day, the bartender stopped showing up to work regularly. She was older and had worked for the business for fifteen years. I couldn't really blame her. Besides, her no-show, no-calls on Mondays and Wednesdays gave me the chance to bring out my inner bartender.

In her absence, I'd create cocktails for my tables based on what diners liked and what would pair well with their meals. The flavors of Thai food—sour, sweet, salty, bitter, and spicy—can be complemented by the right cocktail, and soon

I was creating a secret menu based off of these flavor profiles. I felt invigorated whenever people would ask me for "that one cocktail" I made the last time they were there. It was there at this restaurant, in one of the most unlikely of circumstances, that I discovered my love for food and drink.

Then I moved away to Portland. I left the cocktail creations for my friends at parties and switched gears to food and drink writing.

My knack for giving solid advice on eating and drinking stems from more than experiential gut aches though; it's also backed by years of experience writing about food and drink in Portland.

Over time on the food and drink beat, I discovered that the city's craft distilling scene wasn't getting the attention it deserved. Unlike the city's breweries, its distilleries are still relatively under the radar, though they have been steadily building up a reputation. The city's craft brewery landscape may prevail in sheer taproom numbers and attention from the media, but the city's distilleries measure up in real potency.

This guidebook to the higher proof alcohol made in Portland will help you find your way around town without getting too drunk, lost, or hungover.

What You'll Find

This book was written to be an easy, digestible read—one that you could finish while sipping whiskey. Be sure to read through it before heading out to distilleries.

In the "Background" section I prime you in a bit of recent distillery history, how distilling works, how to taste, and some of the spirits you'll encounter in tasting rooms.

Next, you'll learn about each distillery that either distills in Portland or is part of Distillery Row.

What you will find in the book and out tasting is that while some distilleries may have similar products, they all differ in what they offer in terms of taste, nose, price, and aging methods.

Portland distilling and spirits production is impacted by what happens outside of the city's boundaries too. Explore distilleries all over Oregon (and in faraway North Portland) in the "Beyond" section.

After you've familiarized yourself with Oregon-made spirits, you will want to reference the "After Party Section" for recommendations on Portland's best craft cocktail bars, where to buy locally made supplies to stock your home bar—and if you should drink in excess—some of Portland's best bartenders have provided guidance on surviving the aftermath.

When you are done with this guidebook, keep it as a coaster on your nightstand or hand it off to a Portland newbie in need of insider knowledge. Either way, go to the distilleries in Portland often and leave with many souvenirs, though hopefully not one that lasts well into the next day. Regardless, this is the moment—and the booze—you'll be glad you paid attention to now.

Cheers,
Karen Locke

I.

TASTING

BACKGROUND
& PREP

Y ou're ready to tour some distilleries. Before you do, get grounded in a bit of Portland's distilling history and learn the ettiquette of sipping tasters.

FOOD & DRINK IN PORTLAND

Portland's artisan food and drink scene is one of the best in the nation. We're beloved by national media and tourists alike. In Portland, you don't have to dream about making a living from handmade candy, ice cream, bitters, or hot sauce—you can do it and grow a loyal fan base along with your bank account.

One major reason for this reputation is our exacting standards when it comes to food and drink. We're not snobs, but we often expect nearly every facet of our dining experience to be stunning (and local), up to the dessert fork and until the last swig of our post-dinner coffee. That same loyal fan base is also beginning to care about spirits.

THE FUTURE OF DRINKING IN PORTLAND

The distilling industry in Portland is extensive for any U.S. city (currently under fifteen tasting rooms within city limits) and gaining more traction. We're producing and bottling more brown spirits in the city than in surrounding states combined. We're producing previously foreign-made spirits like aquavit and krupnik in growing numbers. In 2004, there were only ten craft distilleries in the nation, and today we've exceeded that in Bridgetown alone.

Most distillers in Portland will tell you that this is just the beginning—a beginning paved in part by brewing. America's brewing landscape started to change by the late 1970s. That renaissance came about to fill a void. Craft brewers gave consumers what they barely knew they wanted at the time: full-bodied beer. People went from drinking kegs of generic Pilsner-style beer to guzzling microbrews like pale ales, lagers, and IPAs made with depth and varying ingredients.

The path brewers took to ensure that all facets of brewing would be legal in Oregon, including serving beer on-site at the breweries, setting up distribution channels, and so on, didn't go unnoticed by the distilling industry. To some degree, distillers and the Oregon Distillers Guild followed in the footsteps of the brewing industry to ensure that landmark laws were passed.

Distilling in Portland is now making its mark in other ways. While craft brewers have long convinced consumers to desire more variation, craft distillers who want to be creative face an uphill battle to persuade consumers that deviation from old-style standards can be just as desirable. Distilling has long, proud traditions. Think of the liquors that are produced in Scotland (Scotch) and Kentucky (bourbon). People have come to expect distilling to be done in a certain way, and the spirits made in particular locations to have a certain taste and quality. Veering from those classic formulas would be viewed as risky. There are universal truths in distilling, rules to follow. It's widely accepted that whiskey should be made from malted barley and aged at least three years. But what if Portland distillers changed all that?

Distillers here are going down that path already, introducing small changes and tweaks, such as reusing charred barrels, varying barley treatments, or adopting multiple-malt approaches. New distilleries will open and some will close, but the future of drinking in Portland will only mature with expanded, refined offerings. Soon we'll start to see the release of more Portland-made whiskey aged longer than three years. Eventually, more craft distilleries will have the overhead to take on rum, creating products as good as the classics but with a unique Portland stamp. The future is bright for intrepid craft distillers. Portland distilleries have the experience, creative freedom, and resources to continue experimenting in ways the big distilleries can't—or won't.

Whatever Portland distillers dream up, it will hopefully be celebrated as a signature regional style. I predict that the loyal fan base Oregon wine and beer currently possess will happen for Portland-made spirits. We'll see more distilleries opening distillery pubs or adjacent bars for consumers, and creating new ways to present spirits alongside food, cocktails, beer, or wine.

What does this mean for you? In the here and now, go on tours, talk to the distillers, and enjoy the tastings. Take the time to savor the offerings. It's truly one of the best times to fall in love with Portland craft distilling—and it's only going to get better.

A SHORT HISTORY: BRIDGETOWN BEGINNINGS

The 1970s in Oregon were good to winemakers, specifically pinot noir producers, and by the 1980s, the Pacific Northwest had caught the craft beer craze too. Supportive legislation and consumer demand created an environment where both industries could thrive, cultivating Oregon's worldwide reputation and distinction in wine and beer.

The wine and beer industries paved the way for those making the stronger stuff—spirits and liqueur. In 1985, Steve McCarthy started Clear Creek Distillery, the first new distillery to open and operate in Oregon since Prohibition. The inspiration for Clear Creek came while Steve was on a trip abroad. After traveling around Europe, Steve wanted to find a way to recreate the eau de vie and brandy he had tasted, and it just so happened that his family owned a fruit orchard back in Oregon. Experimenting with the local fruit, Steve opened Clear Creek on the corner of NW 23rd Avenue and Quimby Street. The granddaddy of distilling in Portland was about to put Portland on the map. Of the distilleries still around today, New Deal Distillery opened its doors in 2004, and House Spirits Distillery in 2005.

THE 2000S TO THE PRESENT

Fast forward to 2007. Hijinks were real on Alberta Street. The Clown House was losing steam. *Money Magazine* had just named the Pearl District in Northwest Portland one of the best places to retire. Despite the economic turmoil of the Great Recession and the fact that the state had the second highest spirits tax rates in the nation, distilling in Portland was happening. Soon Portlanders started noticing distilleries popping up around town. Distilling had now become "a thing," although not necessarily a topic of conversation.

That same year in 2007, the Oregon Distillers Guild was formed to grow and sustain the burgeoning craft distilling industry through education and legislative action. By 2009, there were eight distilleries operating in the city. Attracted by the cheap rent, more and more distilleries moved into old warehouses in Inner Southeast Portland. Around that same year, the name "Distillery Row" was coined to describe the area on the east side of the Willamette River, south of Interstate 84 and north of Hawthorne Boulevard—now the de facto home to Portland's pioneering distilleries.

DISTILLERY ROW & NW DISTILLER'S DISTRICT

Before Portland distillers started working together to promote their stimulating elixirs, they didn't have common business hours, nor did they promote tastings and events. Some of them didn't even have signs outside their buildings. The rise and development of Distillery Row in Southeast Portland made a travel destination out of an area that few people were exploring at the time and made Portland's craft distillery scene more accessible to the public than ever before. How did the idea for Distillery Row come about? After being inspired by the success of the Kentucky Bourbon Trail (www.kybourbontrail.com) and its Passport program, Highball founder Michael Heavener decided he wanted to do something similar to promote the growth of distilleries in Portland and to raise awareness of the city's craft offerings.

Around the same time, Jupiter Hotel—the revamped mid-century motor hotel in Southeast Portland—started promoting a room package that included a tour of the distilleries in the area. Later, the NW Distiller's District across the Willamette River in Northwest Portland was added to

DISTILLERY TASTING ROOM OPENINGS

DISTILLERY ROW:

2004 - New Deal Distillery

2005 - House Spirits Distillery

2008 - Eastside Distilling

2009 - Vinn Distillery
    - Stone Barn Brandyworks

2012 - Rolling River Spirits

2014 - Wild Roots Vodka

2015 - Thomas & Sons Distillery

NW DISTILLER'S DISTRICT:

1985 - Clear Creek Distillery

2010 - Bull Run Distilling Company

2015 - Martin Ryan Distilling Company (began distilling in 2012)

NORTH PORTLAND:

2011 - Industrial Row Distillery

the Distillery Row Passport program. All distilleries within the two respective areas—Distillery Row and NW Distiller's District—are located less than half a mile's walk (or stagger) from one another. The buzz around Portland's distilling scene was getting louder.

OREGON DISTILLERS GUILD & THE OREGON DISTILLERY TRAIL

In 2013, the Oregon Distillers Guild launched the Oregon Distillery Trail (www.oregondistillerytrail.com) as an online promotional guide to distilleries in the state. The Guild formed in 2007 with intentions to represent and "further the post Prohibition legislative agenda, all in order to sustain and build [the] thriving craft spirits industry." The Guild continues to build public awareness by supporting events such as the Great American Distillers Festival and TOAST, a spirits tasting event in Portland.

OREGON LIQUOR CONTROL COMMISSION

The Oregon Liquor Control Commission (OLCC) controls the distribution, sales, and consumption of alcohol in the state of Oregon. It sets the ground rules—no, the OLCC isn't the bad guy—and this means certain limits are established for consumers and businesses that make and sell liquor. For example, we can only buy hard liquor at state-owned liquor stores. The bars we patronize have to serve us food while we drink. If we want to serve booze as a bartender, we have to get a service permit that ensures we know how to cut people off when they've had too much to drink and resist the urge to drink ourselves while on the job.

Distilleries can get a separate license from the OLCC that would allow them to sell and serve cocktails, but this also means distilleries have to provide food service at all times while cocktails are being served. Basically, if a distillery wants to serve full-size drinks in its tasting room, it's required to have a license, full kitchen, and dining service.

MADE IN PORTLAND VS. DISTILLED IN PORTLAND

This might be a surprising revelation: spirits that are "bottled" and "produced" in Portland may not necessarily be distilled here. Some alcohol like whiskey and bourbon are blended and bottled at a particular distillery—but not necessarily distilled there. This can happen for many reasons, primarily because it's more economical for the purveyor. Reputable distillers are usually honest and transparent about which products are actually distilled in Portland and which are just bottled or produced here. You'll know the difference if you read the labels carefully. As you can imagine, a hyper-local city like Portland wants its spirits to be as local as possible.

Here's another way to think about it: Consider the coffee you drink in Portland. It may be roasted and bagged in Portland by a local company, but the beans are probably from Colombia or another coffee-producing region. If a coffee roaster didn't tell you where the beans were from, but you knew it was roasted here in Bridgetown, you probably wouldn't assume the beans are from here, too, because, well, that would be fairly impossible.

With distilleries, the assumptions you can make about

the products aren't as clear-cut. When it comes to spirits and other types of alcohol, unless it's explicitly stated on the labeling, it's nearly impossible to tell if the liquor was actually distilled in Portland without a look inside the distillery. So, you largely depend on the distiller to be upfront in its labeling and marketing. Luckily, transparency is the norm in the industry here, and labels are generally clear and honest about what's produced here versus what's distilled here. Sourcing isn't uncommon in the distilling world, particularly for whiskey and bourbon, where the barrels have to sit, collecting dust, for around two to four years before bottling.

Whether or not "grain-to-bottle" is an important factor depends on the individual buyer. One thing is certain: whether they are made here (distilled here) or merely bottled and produced here, these brands are truly Portland and worth supporting. Just don't forget to read the label before getting into a finicky debate at the bar.

PRODUCTS OF THE ENVIRONMENT

Regional ingredients inevitably have their own unique flavor profiles—their own signature terroir. Terroir (pronounced tare-WAHr) is a term used by wineries to denote how a region's climate, soil, and terrain impact the taste of the wine. Like wineries, breweries take into account terroir, too; ingredients like the water and hops used in the brewing process impart a regional imprint on the resulting beer. It's no different for distilleries. The malted barley, corn flour, or regional weather conditions where barrels are made and stored affect the flavor of the vodka, whiskey, or gin produced.

Portland food and drink purveyors, including distillers, work together to create products that truly reflect the land and region from where they're derived. It's not difficult to find products here where nearly all of the ingredients are grown, harvested, or sourced in Oregon or nearby Washington. For distillers, knowing locality is important because it often makes sense economically. Many distillers have close relationships with growers, in addition to the wine and beer industries. Distillers often procure barrels previously used for beer or wine for special projects.

HOW TO BE AN EXPERT SPIRITS TASTER

Does it seem like there are some unknowns to distillery tasting? Maybe it's your first time, or perhaps you're just not sure about tasting room etiquette. You're not alone.

I have a friend who has a theory: if you walk into any public establishment wearing a boilersuit or coveralls while whistling, you can get away with anything. (Just imagine being able to leave a 7-Eleven with a Slurpee machine unscathed!) The

Quick and Dirty: How Distilling Works

Distilling, or the production of spirits, happens in two stages: fermentation and distillation. Fermentation is the stage where the alcohol is created, while distillation is the stage where the alcohol is separated and removed.

Before distilling begins, the grain must be first turned into a mash to convert the starches to simple sugars. Water is added to the grain and cooked. The end result tastes almost like a liquid blended from unsweetened oatmeal. The mash is then fermented. Yeast is added to break down the sugars into alcohol and carbon dioxide.

Next, the mash is distilled. The mixture is heated in a still, vaporizing the alcohol and separating out the water and grain particles. The vaporized alcohol is later cooled or condensed to form clear drops of liquid—the spirits—that's later collected.

Ageing and blending can happen next, depending on the spirit, before it's eventually bottled.

point is this: it's all about perception and how you carry yourself. With the right attitude, you can go from curious novice to experienced taster in no time. (Just don't practice my friend's theory and show up in a uniform to rob the place.)

Since you'll be working on confidence and mindset, it's important not to underestimate the power of the thimble-sized shots served at distilleries. With the easy-to-follow guidelines in this chapter, you can have an enjoyable tasting and possibly a hangover-free next day.

PREP WELL: MIND OVER GUT

Theories on how to combine or drink your libations abound. We all remember the saying, "Beer before liquor, never been sicker; liquor before beer, you're in the clear." There's also that theory that you shouldn't drink red wine before hard liquor.

After attending a lot of events as a drink writer, where mixing liquors is the norm, I've discovered that you really can drink any combination of spirits imaginable—if you take a few precautions. While you're still creating a cement mixer in your gut, you might not have to send out an apology text to your friends that next morning by following these rules.

Take the rule everyone knows: Drink in moderation. The more hangovers we conquer, the more we tell ourselves that pacing and moderation matter the most. Yes, moderation definitely plays a part. But it's also more than that. While how much and how fast you drink affects the impact of alcohol on the body, avoiding a night of regret also has a lot to do with the quality of liquor you're drinking, as well as the amount. Lucky for you, distilleries in Portland make high-quality liquors that are served to you in very small quantities!

Next, consider alcohol absorption. Your body doesn't care

if you just mixed coffee liqueur and whiskey. It only cares that you've eaten a meal beforehand and are hydrated. Drinking on a full stomach can regulate the buzz and staying hydrated will ease wicked hangovers later.

Finally, take into account your personal stats and fitness as well. Weight and metabolism play big factors; some people feel the boozy effects sooner, and it's no different when you're drinking thimble-sized shots. Hey, it's not your fault if you're a lightweight. Just know your personal limits and adjust your drinking accordingly!

Remember, distillery tasting is just as potent as a night out drinking, if not more, especially if you take my advice and head to other bars after your tastings. The distilleries may be serving only sips, but it's best not to gloss over the power of those tiny shots.

Let's recap:
- Eat a solid meal beforehand, preferably foods with a good amount of protein and fat. (Think burger and fries, not carrot and celery sticks.)
- Drink plenty of water and try to stay hydrated while you drink.
- Sip your alcohol slowly. (Remember, you're here to savor and taste, not pound the shots).
- And don't forget: convince someone to be your DD, or designated driver, if you plan to travel by car.

So, get that mix of firewater churning without trepidation. Once you get over your fear of the effects of certain liquors, you'll open up so many doors to amazing cocktails and tastings.

KNOW WHAT YOU'RE DRINKING

Each distillery featured in this book has a portfolio of many types of liquors. Here's a breakdown of the spirits you might find:

AQUAVIT

star anise

This Scandinavian spirit is a neutral spirit, flavored with botanicals and distilled from grain. The main flavor is caraway seed, which is balanced with other flavors like anise, citrus, coriander, cumin, dill, fennel, juniper, or star anise.

BRANDY

A strong spirit distilled from wine or fermented fruit juice. The brandies made in Portland are fresh and dry.

EAU DE VIE

This generally colorless and super dry brandy is made by fermenting fruit rather than distilling that fermented fruit into a fruit mash.

FLAVORED LIQUORS

This category runs the gamut from coffee-based and tea-based liqueur to fruit-based liqueur. Liqueurs are made using distillation, extraction, or infusion methods.

GIN

Gin is distilled from grains and commonly gets its piney flavor from juniper berries, although many distilleries in Portland use other botanicals in addition to juniper. Central and Eastern Oregon's climate is perfect for growing juniper, and much of the gin distilled in Oregon uses these local berries.

juniper

GRAPPA & OUZO

Grappa is made by taking the skins, pulp, seeds, and stems leftover from wine production. Ouzo is produced the same way and flavored with anise.

RUM

When most people think of rum, they think of the spiced, syrupy headache called a Rum and Coke cocktail. Rum is made from a sugarcane byproduct like molasses. Rum ranges from silver (white) to amber (dark). Most rum is great in cocktails, but if you're looking to sip straight, find rum aged more than two years, preferably five years. Aged rum has more complex flavor notes like caramel, vanilla, or tobacco.

VODKA

Consisting of water and ethanol, vodka is made from fermented grains or potatoes. Distilleries often start with runs of vodka because it's cheaper and takes less time to produce than whiskey or rum.

WHISKEY

Whiskey is made from a fermented mash of grains like rye or corn. The difference in the type of whiskey produced depends on the grain. Bourbon whiskey has to be made from at least fifty-one percent corn. Because whiskey takes time to barrel age, many distilleries in Portland are just now releasing bottles. Some distilleries will only finish a whiskey. The spirit isn't actually distilled in the facility, only finished there.

BLURRED LINES

Most craft distillers in Portland work with and produce what they can, using available, locally grown ingredients. The spirits snapshot we have for Portland includes what distilleries here are making.

While you won't find tequila or Scotch made in Portland, some lines are blurred for other kinds of liquors. For example, take grappa. Italian law says that only grappa produced either in Italy, in the Italian part of Switzerland, or in San Marino can be officially called grappa. But grappa made in Portland is called grappa nonetheless and sold as grappa.

LEARN TO TASTE LIKE AN EXPERT

Now that we've touched on the types of spirits you're bound to encounter in Portland, you'll want to know the basic rules of distillery hopping before you go on your tasting tour. Avoid that awkward moment of holding booze in your mouth for too long, or throwing back a spirit like you're in your grandparents' basement. Instead, learn to drink like the true spirits sophisticate that you are (or strive to be).

> No. 1 < *Take your time.*

Only a few distilleries have tasting rooms with full-size bars where you can pull up and sit down. Most places usually have a simple bar or counter to stand next to, which facilitates popping in for quick tasters. Take your time, though. It might feel awkward drinking with the distillery employee eyeing your every move, but there's no need to blast your shots down one after the other. Go slow. Ask questions between sips. You'll get more out of the experience if you take the time to really taste what's touching your tongue.

> No. 2 < *Spitting is optional.*

At wine tastings, it's not uncommon to see the use of spitting canteens. At beer tastings, spitting out beer samples would usually mean that you didn't like what you tasted. When it comes to spirit tastings, spitting does happen, but it's very rare. Very few people spit; it's like showing up at the all-nude soaking pool in a one-piece swimsuit. You can do it, but you might feel weird.

Everything in a distillery is decided by your nose and taste buds working together. Because of the nature of spirits, they just taste better if swallowed, so the norm is to swallow and just enjoy the taster from start to finish.

Distillers are brave souls, really, and they likely won't judge you for putting back an entire tasting. On the other hand, don't worry if you don't want to finish your shot. No one will be offended if you don't finish your tasting. You can leave the leftover in its little cup on the bar, or you can hand it over to a friend that enjoyed it more than you.

⟩ No. 3 ⟨ *Give it a whiff before you drink.*

First, pick up your taster cup and give it a good whiff. The amount served will be quite small, almost thimble-like. (Don't worry—if you're trying to get drunk, you will.) Give it another whiff. Is the aroma what you expected? Maybe the spirit's flavor notes are smokier or more floral than you assumed. What does the taste remind you of? Make sure your brain, nose, and taste buds work together to make the tasting experience worthwhile. Also, taking a sniff before you drink makes you look like you know what you're doing, and you'll look and feel more confident.

⟩ No. 4 ⟨ *Swallow.*

Take small sips. Let the alcohol settle on your tongue while you exhale through your nose. This enhances the tasting by activating your nose as well as your tongue. Once you swallow, you'll be able to note the aftertaste.

Taking it slow helps you taste smaller amounts and fully process the flavor profile of the liquor. If not downing a shot is a new experience for you and you like it, go ahead and congratulate yourself; you might just be starting down the path of sophisticated sipping.

$\overline{\rangle\ \text{No. 5}\ \langle}$ *Taste with a poker face.*

Spirits are strong stuff. Whether or not you're a fan of what you're drinking, resist the urge to go quickly. Instead, take careful sips. The urge to wrinkle your nose or make a puke face will subside, especially after a few tasters in. Before you know it, you'll be tasting with a straight face without any effort at all.

$\overline{\rangle\ \text{No. 6}\ \langle}$ *Tip the distillery employee.*

If there's an obvious container or jar for tips at the bar, tip the distillery employees or distillers. While they might not be mixing you fancy martinis with Castelvetrano olives, more than likely they'll be indulging your questions or walking you through the tasting process. They may give you a rundown of the company's entire portfolio or tell you about distillery production. More importantly, they'll often advise you on the best way to drink their spirits. Take their advice on what spirits to drink and in what order (yes, the tasting sequence matters if you don't want to wreck your palate). Before you leave, don't forget to get recommendations on cocktail recipes that you can make at home. And even if there isn't a tip jar, and you want to tip them, be generous and go for it—it'll likely be appreciated.

$\overline{\rangle\ \text{No. 7}\ \langle}$ *Bring cash (or credit card) to buy booze to take home.*

Tastings at distilleries are usually $10 or less, which makes it cash friendly. The number of tasters you get depends on the distillery, and some tastings even include mini cocktails.

You've finished. Do you like what you've tasted? Are you thrilled about the distillery and the people who run it? Show your appreciation by buying a bottle of that rum, liqueur, or vodka you just tried. Cash is easier for tastings, but most places will have a credit card reader in case you spend all of your funds along the way or want to make bigger purchases. Buying something during your tour is the best way to support the purveyor.

OTHER WAYS TO PREPARE BEFORE YOU GO ON A TOUR

Here are some final words of advice for when you go on your distillery adventure:

- Craft a just-in-case apology text that reads something like this: "Sorry about last night. I don't remember breaking your IKEA coffee table after we got back to your place, but…" Save it as a draft and be prepared to modify it based on the recipient and/or your behavior.

- Purchase a Portland Distillery Passport for discounts on tastings at distilleries in Distillery Row and NW Distiller's District.

- Bring along *High-Proof PDX*. Use the "Notes" section to keep track of your likes and dislikes and other thoughts and epiphanies during your tour.

- Consider bringing along a tote bag or backpack to carry your liquor purchases. While carrying around a bottle of booze in a brown paper bag is common in Portland, it also makes some bartenders nervous if you walk into their bar while brown bagging it.

- Arrange for transportation ahead of time. Have the information of several cab companies ready in your phone contacts list, or have ride-share apps downloaded, just in case. Remember, local transportation companies can book up fast, especially in the summer months.

DISTILLERY ROW

EASTSIDE DISTILLING

HOUSE SPIRITS DISTILLERY

NEW DEAL DISTILLERY

ROLLING RIVER SPIRITS

STONE BARN BRANDYWORKS

THOMAS & SONS DISTILLERY

VINN DISTILLERY

WILD ROOTS VODKA

EASTSIDE DISTILLING

TASTING ROOM:
1512 SE 7th Avenue • (503) 926-7060
Sunday-Thursday, 12 noon-8 pm;
Friday-Saturday, 12 noon-10pm

EXECUTIVE OFFICES & DISTILLERY
1805 SE Martin Luther King Boulevard
(971) 888-4264
www.eastsidedistilling.com

At a glance⟶ Portland's emporium of rum, whiskey, and flavored spirits. There's something for everyone here.

Founded by⟶ Lenny Gotter.

What's in a name?⟶ Inspired by Lenny Gotter's love for Portland's Eastside neighborhoods.

Tasting room vibes⟶ Roomy. Choose from three different bars in a room where distilling once happened.

Year opened⟶ 2008.

Tours⟶ None at the SE 7th Avenue tasting room location; distillery operations are now located at 1805 SE Martin Luther King Boulevard.

How to know you've arrived⟶ You'll be surrounded by industrial business-to-business warehouses that offer a range of goods and services, plus a few restaurants.

FROM A VACATION COCKTAIL TO A PROFESSION

There's a certain kind of euphoria that comes over us when we drink cocktails on vacation, or really any alcoholic beverage for that matter. It goes beyond getting very drunk because we don't have to go to work on Monday. That caipirinha you ordered a thousand miles from home was memorable, sure, but we know we likely can't recreate the setting, mood, or fine craftsmanship that went into producing it. Yet that doesn't stop us. We come up with ideas and plans to recreate that experience back home anyway.

This is what happened to Lenny Gotter, the owner and founder of Eastside Distilling. While on vacation in 2006, relaxing on the beaches of Belize and drinking a rum cocktail, Lenny Gotter had an epiphany: people in Portland needed to experience this rum. It occurred to him that liquor stores back in the States didn't have a comparable rum selection. Much of what was available back home—big brand-name spirits like Bacardi, Malibu, and Captain Morgan—were approachable and affordable but also flavored and rarely aged.

It was obvious to Lenny that the American palate needed rum as good as the rum he enjoyed in Belize. Initially, Lenny thought maybe he would import rum and introduce it to Portlanders that way. He knew very little about distilling, but as the taste of the rum lingered, he thought, Why not distill the rum myself?

Was it a crazy leap of faith to produce a rum made in the Pacific Northwest—or was it just the rum talking?

By 2009, Lenny was back in the States and trying his hand at distilling his own rum in Portland. From there, he moved on to other spirits. For Lenny, in the distilling business, "the beautiful part is seeing what you end up with."

Eastside Distilling continues to dream up new creations, although it continues to produce different styles of rum: silver, ginger, coffee, and spiced. Burnside Bourbon may be one of Eastside Distilling's most recognizable spirits, but the company's portfolio also includes other bespoke flavors, such as Oregon Oaked Bourbon and Cherry Bomb Whiskey, in addition to spirits like the Marionberry Whiskey or Holiday Spiced Liqueur, which can be sipped or mixed in cocktails. Eastside's range is broad enough that if you only wanted to buy Eastside Distilling products to stock your bar, you'd have nearly everything you needed to start mixing basic cocktails.

Master distiller, Melissa Heim, is one of the few female distillers in the industry and the first female to distill west of the Mississippi. Melissa joined Eastside Distilling in 2012 after an apprenticeship and run as a head distiller at Rogue Distillery and Public House is Northwest Portland. Humbly working her way up, Melissa accepted a job with Eastside Distilling as a labeler, then tour guide, assistant next, then production lead and then master distiller.

In 2016, Melissa was appointed Executive Vice President, making her the senior-most operational manager at the company.

TASTING TIPS: GETTING THE MOST OUT OF YOUR VISIT

Taste the spirits in the order recommended by the tasting room employer or the stronger flavored spirits and liqueurs may be all you'll taste for the duration of your visit. Don't forget to try a mini cocktail prepared in the distillery tasting room.

◆ Tasting Menu ◆

Holiday liqueur: Egg Nog 'Advocaat' Liqueur, Holiday Spiced Liqueur, Peppermint Bark Liqueur

Rum: Below Deck Coffee Rum, Below Deck Ginger Rum, Below Deck Silver Rum, Below Deck Spiced Rum

Vodka: Portland Potato Vodka

Whiskey: Barrel Hitch American Whiskey, Barrel Hitch Oregon Oak American Whiskey, Burnside

Bourbon, Cherry Bomb Whiskey, Marionberry Whiskey, Oregon Oaked Bourbon

High-Proof pick: Definitely try the Barrel Hitch Oregon Oak American Whiskey. The grainy and earthy taste is sure to please. There's a bit of spice in there too—cardamom—in addition to honeycomb.

HOUSE SPIRITS DISTILLERY

TASTING ROOM:
65 SE Washington Street • (503) 235-3174

Daily, 12 noon–6 pm

PDX AIRPORT TASTING ROOM:
Concourse C

www.housespiritsdistillery.com

At a glance—→ A leader in the American craft distilling movement, creator of internationally known and distributed Aviation American Gin. Also, one of the first distilleries in the U.S. to produce aquavit.

Founded by —→ Christian Krogstad and Lee Medoff. (Lee has since left House Spirits and is presently the co-owner of Bull Run Distilling Company.) Fun fact: NFL legend Joe Montana owns a stake in House Spirits.

What's in a name?—→ Christian Krogstad's wife came up with the name as a play on alcoholic spirits and a reference to the folklore of "house spirits" that live in people's homes.

Tasting room vibes——→ An upscale, yet fun environment (they have a photobooth!). It's the perfect place to celebrate contemporary cocktail culture.

Year opened——→ 2004 in Corvallis, Oregon; opened a location in Portland in 2005.

Tours——→ Monday-Friday at the top of the hour, 1pm-5pm; Saturdays, 1pm and 3pm; Sundays, 3pm. Tours are $20 per person and include tastings.

How to know you've arrived——→ From the back, House Spirits Distillery looks like many of the warehouses in the area. If you're winding your way around the Southeast Portland Riverfront District, look for the bright yellow Olympic Mills Commerce Center building next door. The doors to the tasting room are just off of Washington Street with access from the parking lot.

TURNING BEER INTO SPIRITS

Distilling and brewing have strong similarities: both start with a process of malting, or soaking the grain in water to sprout the grain. They both involve mashing, or converting the starches into soluble sugars, to make alcohol. Finally, both undergo fermentation. If you think about it, whiskey is essentially distilled beer. Distillers start by turning the grain into beer (not drinkable by most standards), and then continue the distillation to make whiskey.

These similarities in techniques allow brewers to become distillers and vice versa. Sometimes brewers gravitate to the particular creativity that comes with distilling and never turn back. There's more potential to produce vastly different products like bourbon and vodka in spirits distilling. There are also opportunities to modify centuries-old recipes and get away with it. For example, the process of aging in distilling allows distillers to influence the flavor post-creation. All this extra room for ingenuity often gets brewers distilling. Original co-founders of House Spirits Distillery, Christian Krogstad and Lee Medoff, took this beer-to-spirits route.

The two met as brewers at McMenamins, a chain with now sixty-five brewpubs, multiple breweries, music venues, historic hotels, and theater pubs throughout the region. Their careers making brews there in the late 1990s took a turn toward whiskey when McMenamins opened the doors to its distillery in 1998. Lee was enlisted to help develop the process and from that day continued the distillate process of turning "beer" into whiskey.

Before House Spirits, Christian managed the Carlton Winemakers Studio in Carlton, Oregon, a green-focused winery cooperative of independent small-batch winemakers in the Yamhill area of Oregon known as Oregon's wine capital. He also founded and managed Orchard Street Brewery in Bellingham, Washington. Years later, he became a brewer at McMenamins where he met Lee.

Lee describes the process of starting House Spirits as "putting together a business on a shoestring." That meant starting out with very little funds and resources. The knowledge of distilling in the Pacific Northwest in the mid-2000s was limited to other distillers who had already scraped together the knowledge and the funds to start a distillery. Even today there are very few publications and how-to guides on starting your own distilling business.

During the time Christian and Lee ran House Spirits Distillery together, several staple products were developed, including Medoyeff Vodka, a European-style grain-forward vodka (now made by Bull Run Distilling Company, and Aviation American Gin, a batch-distilled American-style gin.) With Medoyeff Vodka, Lee wanted a spirit that would honor his Russian heritage, specifically a quality craft vodka that his own grandfather would drink and appreciate and have good reason never to buy another vodka brand ever again. After Lee left House Spirits Distillery in 2010 to start Bull Run Distilling Company, with a focus on whiskey and bourbon, Medoyeff Vodka moved with him.

TAKING OFF WITH AVIATION AMERICAN GIN

Much of House Spirits's reputation is due to its best-selling product, Aviation American Gin. With distribution and sales as far flung as Hong Kong, Aviation Gin is well recognized on the shelf even by the casual cocktail connoisseur. Yet despite its popularity, this craft gin is still produced in-house and in small batches in Portland.

The serendipitous origins of Aviation American Gin can be traced back to a bartender in Seattle (now a Portlander), Ryan Magarian, who happened to get a taste of a mysterious bottle of "botanical infusion" that crossed his hands. An instant fan, Ryan later tracked down the bottle's origins to House Spirits in Portland. He and Christian started talking. Eventually, the bartender-distiller team agreed to work together to refine the booze. They ran nearly thirty trials before they came up with the final recipe for what would later become Aviation American Gin. In 2016, House Spirits sold Aviation Gin to Davos Brands. House Spirits is still the sole contracted distiller and produces the gin but is no longer owner. Why sell such a beloved spirit? The sale gave House Spirits the bandwidth to focus on its whiskey: Westward Oregon Straight Malt Whiskey.

THE BIG MOVE

What would you do with a cool $6 million? How about devote an entire room of your beloved mansion to rare bottles of whiskey salvaged from sunken ships found at the bottom of the ocean, and then decorate the walls with paintings of monkeys in tuxedos? (Well, that's what I'd do at least.)

Some dreams really do come true. House Spirits's distillers did just that, though without the monkeys in tuxedos and with their own craft-made spirits, of course. In 2015, House Spirits moved from its old location on 7th Avenue and opened the doors at their current location on SE Washington Street to the tune of $6 million. At fourteen thousand square feet, it's now one of the largest distilleries in Oregon. House Spirits is still included in the marketing efforts of Distillery Row even after the move to Washington Street.

The interiors of House Spirits's new tasting room were designed with the help of Andee Hess of Osmose Design, the design eye behind Salt & Straw, a popular artisan ice cream shop, Stumptown, the coffee that put Portland on the map, and Ava Gene's, a contemporary, hip Italian restaurant, as well as other Portland institutions. Inside House Spirits's lavish building, you'll first notice the gorgeous backlit shelving featuring the company's prized booze. It's a truly beautiful, glamorous sight, a veritable monument of spirits, complete with the perfect glowing light to give everything that aura. Stand there for a moment and take in this exquisite oasis of booze. Elaborate art deco details, a few inspired by the Aviation American Gin bottle's curved edges, can be found all over the walls and shelving and around the bar.

MORE ROOM FOR WHISKEY

The distillery's relocation allowed House Spirits to produce more, particularly more of one of its favorites, Westward Single-Barrel Oregon Straight Whiskey (www.westwardwhiskey.com).

Those American oak barrels take up a lot of space as they sit and mature, and the added space allows House Spirits to make and age more of it. Good thing, too. Westward is very special: a whiskey made from one hundred percent malted barley grown in the Pacific Northwest and fermented with ale yeast. It's then double pot distilled and aged in two-char American oak barrels.

TASTING TIPS: GETTING THE MOST OUT OF YOUR VISIT

Behind the bar, a large viewing window allows visitors to peek at the production process, including the giant stills where the aquavit, gin, vodka, and whiskey are made. Get a front seat to the action while mingling over tasting cups and mini cocktails.

Put your trust in the tasting room guide who will direct you down the right path for tasting House Spirits's libations in an intelligent fashion. Take the advice on the order of the tastings. For example, you'll want to try the aquavit last for good reason. It's pungent and will leave a lasting impression on your tongue that could spoil your taste buds for other libations.

Don't forget to try the mini cocktails on draft to experience House Spirits's cocktails as they are intended. In the non-rainy months, check out the patio tables and chairs in front of the distillery. Afterwards, grab lunch at Olympia Provisions and watch passersby mill about in Portland's Central Eastside.

◆ Tasting Menu ◆

Aquavit: Krogstad Festlig Aquavit

Liqueur: House Spirits Coffee Liqueur, House Spirits Creme de Cacao

Rum: House Spirits Katun Rum

Vodka: Volstead Vodka

Whiskey: Westward Oregon Straight Malt Whiskey

High-Proof pick: Looking for an Oregon-made whiskey? Definitely try Westward Oregon Straight Malt Whiskey. Westward is a malt whiskey inspired by the Irish tradition, but crafted in a unique and distinctively American style. Next, don't miss the mini cocktails on tap that change seasonally and showcase the spirits alongside locally made products like bitters and syrups.

New Deal Distillery

TASTING ROOM & DISTILLERY:
900 SE Salmon Street • (503) 234-2513
Wednesday–Sunday, 12 noon–6 pm
www.newdealdistillery.com

At a glance—→ Community-oriented distillery making experimental, innovative spirits that have become solid Portland staples.

Founded by—→ Tom Burkleaux and Matthew Van Winkle.

What's in a name?—→ Refers to the New Deal government programs enacted from 1933 to 1938 during the

Great Depression.

Tasting room vibes⟶ Open and bright. It's great for large groups.

Year opened⟶ 2004.

Tours⟶ Group tours are available by appointment. Call ahead to schedule.

How to know you've arrived⟶ Look for New Deal's white sign and garage door of windows. The area near the distillery, like much of Distillery Row, has a slew of industrial and manufacturing warehouses.

MAKING IT SIMPLE

Tom Burkleaux and Matthew Van Winkle were living in an apartment together in Southeast Portland for a few years when they decided to venture into distilling. When they opened New Deal Distillery in 2004, there were only ten craft distilleries in the nation.

Many distilleries start out making vodka because it's economical, and then move on to gin and whiskey later. While New Deal eventually took this route, Tom and Matthew started distilling vodka with the specific goal of making better vodka. They had a simple plan in mind when they first opened for business: to sell one bottle of vodka to a stranger off of a liquor store shelf. While this goal might have been modest, their motivations were ambitious. Fed up with a market saturated with high-end, mass-produced "yuppy vodka," as they called it, the distillers sought to make a vodka that got back to the basics. Their motto: "Make it simple, make it right."

A LEARNING PROCESS

For months, Tom and Matthew learned everything they could about the distilling process. They visited the few distilleries they knew like Clear Creek Distillery in Portland. They combed the shelves of Powell's Books for information. Like most craft distilleries, they started with a very loose business plan and experimented repeatedly until the recipes, methods, and planning started falling into place. Immersed in their research, Tom and Matthew chipped away slowly at learning the business, all while balancing full-time day jobs as programmers.

Their first space was small: one hundred and twenty square feet in the ActivSpace arts building on SE Main Street. Knowing they'd need more space, Tom and Matthew eventually moved New Deal across the street, which is where the distillery currently resides. The company has since added a German-made Christian Carl still and a locally made still from Global Stainless based in Canby, Oregon, as well as a new electric bottling line.

If you can make your way back to where the distilling happens, you'll see casually labeled bottles of Tom's "experiments." These are new projects based around loose ideas that might become something final later. It's Tom's style to use his experience to tinker away until something really great happens—usually what goes into the Distiller's Workshop Series. The Series is Tom's experiments released as small-batch brandy, rum, white dog, moonshine, and other specialty craft spirits available only in the tasting room. Try these spirits while you can; they truly are limited and slow to churn out since much of the spirits in the Distiller's Workshop Series takes time to age.

A better way to learn about what New Deal has been working on and to understand the process of distilling is to sign up for one of the distillery's Hands-On Whiskey Making Classes. Classes take place at a table set up in the middle of the distillery, with Tom himself and other New Deal disciples taking you through the process. You'll learn some history while comparing white dogs, help make mash, taste distillate right from the still, and taste spirits already aging in barrels stored at the distillery. Classes take place on Sundays from 10 am to 3 pm. It costs $250 per person and includes morning coffee and lunch.

THE SHARING SPIRIT

New Deal Distillery aims to be more than a good neighbor. It has sponsored hundreds of charitable and cultural organizations throughout Portland in the areas of education, low-income healthcare, youth mentorship, and environmental protection, among others.

Along with charitable work, New Deal has opened its doors over the years to other craft distillers. Part of the distillery's success is also due to the contract distilling it does for smaller producers, which in turn allows Tom to collaborate with others and experiment in new ways. Through the years, Deco Distilling, LOFT Organic Liqueurs, J. Witty Spirits, JVR Spirits, Kachka, and others have used the guidance and expertise offered by New Deal.

New Deal's neighborly gestures have allowed spirits-making individuals and businesses alike to reach wider audiences. Under New Deal's auspices, JVR Spirits creates krupnik, a spiced honey liqueur. Kachka, a Russian restaurant just a few blocks away from the distillery, can now spread its Kachka Horseradish Vodka love, one bottle at a time, instead of by the glass like it does at the restaurant.

TASTING TIPS: GETTING THE MOST OUT OF YOUR VISIT

The space is large and spacious but can get crowded during weekends. To enjoy your tasting experience fully, wait your turn to get to the bar. Yes, it's worth the few-minutes wait to take your time and have a distillery room employee's full attention for questions during your tasting. There's seating by the door and a sign-up sheet for when it's busy.

New Deal Distillery offers an array of rotating mini cocktails for purchase. Don't miss out on these.

◆ Tasting Menu ◆

Distiller's Workshop Series: The Distiller's Workshop Series is New Deal's limited-release, small batch line of spirits. It includes brandy, rum, white dog, and moonshine liquors, such as the following: New Deal Amber Rum, New Deal Brandy, New Deal Rye Whiskey, New Deal Smoked Bourbon Whiskey, Distiller's Cut Rum

Gin: New Deal Gin No. 1, Portland Dry Gin 33

Liqueur: Cascadia American Bitter Liqueur, New Deal Coffee Liqueur, New Deal Ginger Liqueur

Vodka: Hot Monkey Pepper-Flavored Vodka, Mud Puddle Bitter Chocolate Vodka, New Deal Vodka, Portland 88 Vodka

High-Proof pick: Mud Puddle Bitter Chocolate Vodka doesn't really taste like booze on the first sip and consistently gets rave reviews. Also, try a whiskey from the Distiller's Workshop Series. For a fiery infusion of peppers, try New Deal's popular Hot Monkey Vodka, a craft-distilled vodka infused with Southwestern chili peppers. *Tip:* Drink it in a three to one ratio with pineapple juice, neat or over ice, and you have the instant Perfect 31 cocktail.

Rolling River Spirits

TASTING ROOM & DISTILLERY:
1215 SE 8th Ave., Suite H
(503) 235-3174

Monday–Thursday by appointment
Friday–Sunday, 12 noon–5 pm

www.rollingriverspirits.com

At a glance⟶ Spirits influenced by the family's Scandinavian heritage.

Founded by⟶ Husband and wife team Rick Rickard and Joan Rickard, and son Tim Rickard.

What's in a name?⟶ Rolling River refers to the majestic rivers found in the Portland area and the importance of water in the distilling process.

Tasting room vibes⟶ There's a bespoke bar shaped like a seafaring vessel set in the tasting room with views of the distillery's hand-built stills.

Year opened⟶ Started distilling in 2011; opened the Portland tasting room in 2013.

Tours:⟶ Available upon request.

How to know you've arrived⟶ You'll notice 1980s-style warehouses, a few parked cars, low foot traffic, and few people milling about.

Portland has many nicknames: Bridgetown, Stumptown, PDX, and most recently, Transplant City. Transplant City is a newer moniker that reflects the influx of out-of-towners who have steadily moved to Portland over the past ten years, drawn to its relatively affordable housing, laid-back attitude, food and drink culture, and beautiful natural landscapes.

Being homegrown in Portland, or even within a thirty-minute drive of the city, is a special status that not very many people nowadays can claim. Rick and Joan Rickard are from nearby Camas, Washington, while their son Tim Rickard and daughter Elisabeth Rickard are based in Portland proper.

Rolling River Spirits isn't one of those family operations where people are only involved when they have to be involved—like when they're about to inherit the business. The Rickards distill together every day. They show up, share tasks, and finish shifts together. Joan distills and works on recipes. Elisabeth markets the products, creates new cocktail recipes, and works the tasting room floor. Tim and Rick spend most of their days working the stills. All this synchronized teamwork means that they spend a lot of time in each other's company. The result: excellent craft products that reflect not only their heritage but also their dedication to well-made spirits.

Tim, who holds the company title of "Admiral of Distilling," built Rolling River's first still in 2010. Before that, Tim worked for several years as a commissioned artist whose work filled local galleries in Oregon and Washington. Tim's passion for metal sculpture, glass blowing, and three-dimensional art soon shifted to the art of home brewing. By age twenty-one, Tim was happily brewing traditional lagers, porters, and IPAs. Rick himself was making wine around the house too. Then in 2011, the family founded Rolling River Spirits and added craft spirits to the portfolio. The tasting room located on SE 8th Avenue would open about two years later.

The family's first bottled spirit was Rolling River Spirits Vodka, made in a small Continuous Run Reflux Column still, a common still for vodka-making. While many distilleries in Portland purchase stills from manufacturers in Germany or elsewhere, Rolling River produced the family's first product in a still built by hand by Tim himself. For the spirit's label, Tim also created the artwork, which features stately ships rolling down a river.

A BAR FIT FOR A VIKING: CHANNELING THE OLD NORSE SPIRITS
Aquavit is a Scandinavian spirit made with botanicals and distilled from grain. The main flavor is caraway seed, which is balanced with other flavors, such as anise, citrus, coriander, cumin, dill, fennel, juniper, or star anise.

Rolling River Spirits produces Ole Bjørkevoll Aquavit made with caraway, dill, and fennel. In addition, they also produce the Rolling River Spirits Limited Series Stilar, which explores different flavors of aquavits (stilar is Swedish for "styles"). These small, experimental batches are released sparingly, sometimes only once a year. The place to try them is at the distillery tasting room. These one-offs vary from traditional formulas and will delight and surprise.

The Scandinavian ship-inspired bar was built and finished by Tim himself. Around the time the distillery was being built, Tim's friend gave them leftover wood from a nearby lumber mill. Without much of a plan, Tim took the wood pieces and let the material guide his design. Soon a boat started taking shape as he worked on building the bar. After realizing how perfect the parallel was between the Scandinavian spirits like aquavit they'd soon be making and the form the bar had taken on, he kept working on the wood until a hull had fully formed.

When you visit the tasting room at Rolling River, take note of the bar. Even if you aren't nautically inclined (Sperry Top-Siders don't count), you might notice that the bar resembles the hull of a ship, maybe a Viking ship. Stand at the end of the bar and note how the graceful curves bend like the sides of a boat.

TASTING TIPS: GETTING THE MOST OUT OF YOUR VISIT

Spend some time getting to know Rolling River's aquavit. The Norwegian and Scandinavian folks in Oregon are fans, according to Tim. Rolling River also produces more variations of aquavit than any other distillery in Portland.

Rolling River Spirits is part of Distillery Row and close to Eastside Distilling, New Deal Distillery, and Vinn Distillery. For the easiest way to get around, use alternative transportation.

◆ Tasting Menu ◆

Aquavit: Bjørkevoll's Holiday Aquavit, Bjørkevoll's Gamle Holiday Aquavit, Ole Bjørkevoll Aquavit, Old Ole Bjørkevoll Aquavit, Rolling River Spirits Limited Series Stilar

Gin: Rolling River Spirits Gin

Vodka: Coffee Spirit, Habanero Vodka, Rolling River Spirits Vodka, Trinidad Scorpion Vodka (Mild and Hot)

Whiskey: Lost Barrel White Dog

fennel

Stone Barn Brandyworks

TASTING ROOM & DISTILLERY

3315 19 Ave. Suite B • (503) 341-2227

Open weekends, check website for specific
hours and weekday times.

www.stonebarnbrandyworks.com

At a glance⟶ Oregon bounty transformed into an array
of clean barrel aged whiskeys, liqueur, grappa, and, of
course, brandy.

Founded by⟶ Sebastian and Erika Degens

What's in a name?⟶ Inspired by Sebastian Degens's
childhood home.

Tasting room vibes⟶ Newer warehouse filled with
Portland sunlight and jazz sounds in the background.

Year opened⟶ 2009.

Tours⟶ Available upon request. Group tours of six or
ore people are available by appointment. Call ahead to
schedule.

How to know you've arrived⟶ Sandwiched between
SE Powell Boulevard and the Brooklyn Rail Yards' railroad
tracks, the neighborhood where Stone Barn Brandyworks
sits is a mix of warehouses built in the last ten years and
older homes. Stone Barn's location in this industrial part
of the city, nearby other businesses like a European Auto
dealer, various printing presses, a refinisher, and foam

factory, makes it feel secluded, even though it's only a short saunter away from other distilleries on Distillery Row and the rest of Portland civilization.

REKINDLE (OR REDEEM) THOSE MEMORIES

If your first experience with the hard stuff was with a bottle of blackberry brandy in your grandparents' wood-paneled basement with red shag carpeting, you'll appreciate all that Stone Barn Brandyworks has to offer. We might associate brandy with a graying, older crowd, but what Stone Barn is making is far different from the stuffy fruit spirits that you might remember.

Stone Barn makes authentic craft-distilled brandy made with real fruit, as well as brandy-based liqueur and whiskey. If you've sworn off brandy because of a bad experience in the past, get ready to have your impressions of this spirit completely transformed.

BRANDY 101

Brandy tends to be a lot like tequila: a nasty experience in our youth scars us for life, and then we swear off the stuff. In truth, that harsh-tasting bottle you were stealing from Grandpa probably wasn't actual blackberry brandy anyway. Much of America's distaste for brandy comes from the abundance of poorly made brands available to consumers. We drink these inferior liquors, usually chock full of sugar added at bottling, later get a cripplingly memorable hangover, and then swear off the liquor for most of adulthood—until we eventually head to Palm Springs with creaky knees and revert back to the booze that wronged us. There's time enough to enjoy the really good stuff before we all hunker down for cribbage tournaments.

Luckily for Portland, we've got Stone Barn Brandyworks

doing justice for brandy, redeeming bad first experiences with every tipple and proving that brandy isn't just for those headed to retirement.

When we talk about brandy, it can also mean any liquor made from the distillation of pomace, the mash or wine of any fruit. At Stone Barn, you'll notice that the brandy isn't thick or syrupy; rather, it's mostly clear or has a slight golden hue. You'll get a real experience here. The brandy is drinkable, super crisp, and just as intentionally bone dry as the stuff you'll find in Europe.

Grappa is another bewildering spirit for many people. It's a big deal in Italy, where it originated and is as popular as wine, but isn't as popular here in the States. Flavor-wise, it's quite fragrant and boozy. To some, it's mysterious and enigmatic. Grappa isn't so mysterious when you break it down. It's basically a grape-based pomace brandy made by distilling the skins, pulp, seeds, and stems left over from winemaking, usually after the grapes have been pressed. One of the reasons it's not such a big deal here in the U.S.? Badly made grappa. Second-rate grappa—and there's a lot of inferior grappa out there—tastes as harsh as nail polish remover. Finely made grappa, on the other hand, like the stuff made by Stone Barn and other craft distillers, should taste like a potent, concentrated wine.

Now that you've been primed on the qualities of good brandy and grappa, it's time to get over those childhood fears and explore a whole new world of flavors.

NOT YOUR GRANDPARENTS' SPIRITS

Originally from the East Coast, owners Sebastian and Erika Degens moved to Oregon in 1980. Sebastian's German heritage plays a large role in the kinds of spirits distilled at Stone

Barn. Sebastian fondly remembers pear brandy being a part of his own family traditions, and family lore even suggests that his father turned to selling hooch after WWII.

Stone Barn Brandyworks is named for the home Sebastian grew up in. Built in 1806 in Massachusetts, the barn was renovated into a house prior to Sebastian's family purchasing it in the 1960s. You'll find traces of that stone barn if you examine the Stone Barn Brandyworks label. The strip near the bottom of the label that looks like a sliver of a photograph is just that: a photo of a section of the stone barn's wall.

USING OREGON'S BOUNTY

The couple's penchant for working with fruit goes beyond Sebastian's heritage. Sebastian and Erika have always loved the production around working with fruit, from the preparing and drying of fruit, to the preserving and fermenting. Fruit happens to be the heart of a good brandy, the necessary ingredient in forging authentic spirits. In fact, one of the first spirits Stone Barn produced was a plum brandy made from regional fruit.

After dreaming of starting a business together, and because of a shared love for fresh, local produce, and brandy practically being in Sebastian's blood, Sebastian and Erika decided they wanted to open a distillery. While on a bike ride through the Southeast Portland industrial area one afternoon, they noticed a building for lease and the landlord doing work on it. Curious, they stopped to talk to him and began asking him about the property. (In trademark Portland fashion, business deals are often initiated in this way.) One thing led to another, and Stone Barn Brandyworks was born.

In the beginning, Sebastian and Erika started distilling using a stainless steel cauldron they received from a man (fondly referred to as "Frank the Clean-Up Guy") who made indus-trial cleaners and owned a building across the alley. Making things from scratch is important to the company, as is building personal relationships. Sebastian and Erika always make an ef-fort to know everyone they deal with, growers and purveyors alike. Sometimes they see the rhubarb grower at the farmer's market. They personally know the cranberry grower whose berries they use in their liqueurs. This personal touch is dis-tinctively Portland and is what makes Stone Barn spirits so authentic.

BEYOND FRUIT

Working as closely as they do with seasonal fruits, Sebastian and Erika quickly knew Oregon bounty wasn't going to be plentiful year around, so they began producing other spirits, particularly whiskey. For Stone Barn, whiskey may have start-ed as an alternative product for when fruit was hard to come by and fruit spirits and brandy couldn't be made, but it has since become one of Stone Barn's many fine sippable spirits.

TASTING TIPS: GETTING THE MOST OUT OF YOUR VISIT

Finding Stone Barn Brandyworks can be tricky because of its location tucked back off of SE Powell Boulevard. (Keep that in mind if it's your last stop on a voyage to more than one distillery.)

Once you arrive, walk right in, and based on availability, pull up a stool at the tasting room bar. Someone will likely be tending a whiskey mash nearby. Depending on the day, you may see bottling, fermenting, or any other step in the distilling process happen right before your eyes.

Stone Barn's portfolio differs greatly in flavor and potency depending on the season, so try tasting the spirits in the order recommended. For example, don't spoil your taste buds by trying the coffee liqueur first.

Fruit is Stone Barn's specialty. Taste mindfully as fruit flavors can be delicate and subtle. Take a big whiff of that pear liqueur and let it rest on your tongue for a moment. Does it remind you of the pear tree in your grandmother's front yard? That's just what Sebastian and Erika are hoping to do—spark a sweet memory from childhood with an evocative taste. (But if a flavor reminds you of a dusty snifter from your grandparents' basement bar, that's okay too.)

♦ Tasting Menu ♦

Brandy: Bartlett Pear Brandy, Northwest Plum Brandy (barrel-aged)

Fruit variety: Biggs Junction Apricot Liqueur, Cranberry Liqueur, Oregon Blush Rhubarb Liqueur, Quince Liqueur, Nocino (green walnut liqueur), Star Crimson Pear Liqueur, Coffee Liqueur, Tawny Duet (a blend of Pinot Noir dessert wine and Pinot Noir brandy) *Note: Spirits made from the fruit variety don't change but are cycled through based on seasonal availability. Call to ask about current stocks or planned production.*

Grappa and Ouzo: Eastside Ouzo, Malbec Grappa, Ouzo, Pinot Noir Barrel-Aged Grappa

Whiskey: Variety of barrel aged whiskeys. Heavy on the rye, but also variations of oat, spelt, and barley malts.

High-Proof pick: Depending on whether you want to sip or mix, Stone Barn has many stellar options. For sipping, I recommend bringing home a bottle of the

cranberry

distillery's currently available barrel aged whiskey. The fruit spirits aren't overpowering, and you can easily mix one of them in a complex cocktail, along with other ingredients or stronger liquors. For example, make an easy and tasty cocktail using its Quince Liqueur, or Rhubarb Liqueur, combined with other liquors and soda water or sparkling wine.

THOMAS & SONS DISTILLERY

TASTING ROOM & DISTILLERY:
4211 SE Milwaukie Ave • (503) 477-6137

Wednesday–Friday 4pm–7pm
Saturday–Sunday 12 noon–7pm

www.thomasandsonsdistillery.com

At a glance—➤ Innovative tea-based liqueur by the makers of Townshend Tea and Brew Dr. Kombucha.

Founded by—➤ Matt Thomas

What's in a name?—➤ Taken from the owner's last name, Thomas. Also, a tribute to Matt Thomas's young sons.

Tasting room vibes—➤ A classy drinking parlour tucked in the corner of a warehouse. It feels like you're inside a clandestine speakeasy.

Year opened—➤ 2015

Tours⟶ None. Instead, just peep at the equipment before entering the tasting room. Free tastings for patrons are available every month at the Townshend Tea Teahouse on 3531 SE Division Street. Check social media for dates and times.

How to know you've arrived⟶ The block of SE Milwaukie Avenue that Thomas & Son calls home is sparsely inhabited. Head south on Milwaukie, and you'll soon encounter the Sellwood neighborhood's cornucopia of antique shops, taverns, sushi restaurants, and other retail establishments.

BRINGING BACK THE CASUAL VIBE

The story of Thomas & Sons starts with tea. Matt Thomas first started the plan for Townshend's Tea Company in 2002 as an assignment for an MBA class at the University of Oregon. The assignment was to target an underserved market. Matt's plan was to recreate the atmosphere of a casual college campus-style coffeehouse using top-notch loose-leaf tea rather than coffee.

At the time, there were plenty of coffee shops to choose from but no similar establishments with a focus on tea. Townshend's Tea would soon fill that void. Townshend's Tea has hundreds of tea and herbal tea-based offerings, from the classics like green and black teas, to chai, medicinal teas, rare infusions, and bubble tea. It currently has five locations around Oregon, in Portland, Bend, and Eugene, and one location in Bozeman, Montana.

KOMBUCHA CULTURE

In Portland, kombucha is a rite of passage for yuppies, New Age folks, skaters—and everyone in between. Kombucha is a fermented tea made using black or green tea, bacteria, and yeast. The "symbiotic colony of bacteria and yeast," or SCOBY, is the disgusting glob that ferments the tea and makes kombucha possible. If you've seen a SCOBY, you know how gross it is; if you haven't, drink on and don't think about it. Regarded as a probiotic beverage, kombucha is reputed to aid with digestion and improve gut health. It's not unusual to witness a "kombucha date," a social practice where one sips kombucha with a companion. Some bars in Portland now offer kombucha on tap alongside beers.

Townshend's Tea's expansion to kombucha seemed like a natural transition. It fit Matt's mindset of expanding into untapped markets and his desire to showcase tea with different approaches. Kombucha was just another expression of tea that could be poured from the taps of bars around town. Matt realized that people in Portland were talking about kombucha and drinking kombucha. It was time to make some SCOBY-filled batches.

THREE BRANDS STEEPED IN TEA

Townshend's Tea, Brew Dr. Kombucha, and Thomas & Sons may be different brands, but they're all made by the same virtuosos. Buy any Brew Dr. and Thomas & Sons product, and you'll notice that the Townshend's Tea branding is prominently displayed on the labels.

Brew Dr. Kombucha is available in a variety of flavors: Citrus Hops, Clear Mind, Nutritonic, Superberry, Happiness, Spiced Apple, Lemon Ginger Cayenne, Love, Ginger Turmeric. You can buy the bottles at coffee shops, grocery stores, and corner stores, even 7-Elevens, around Portland.

FROM CRUNCHY TO SPEAKEASY

After producing leading, top-quality kombucha, Matt decided it was time to start using tea for something less healthful and more boozeful: delicious alcoholic spirits.

By 2014, Portlanders were hearing rumors in the media about Townshend's Tea expanding from tea and kombucha to tea-based spirits. Once again, the tea company was expanding to fill a void: tea-based spirits.

Matt appointed longtime Townshend's Tea employee Seth O'Malley as the head distiller to lead the company's new distilling operations. Seth began working for Townshend's Tea in 2009 in Bend, Oregon. After he moved to Portland, he first worked at the Alberta Street location, slinging tea there, before moving to the Milwaukie Avenue location. Although distilling was new to him, Seth used his ample experience with tea and knowledge of botanicals to launch tea-centric flavor combinations like Smoke Tea, Spice Tea, and Sweet Tea.

TEA-BASED SPIRITS

Normally, when we think of liqueurs we think of classics like blackberry liqueur, Cointreau, Grenadine, or Grand Marnier—those bottles of booze we buy to make that one cocktail at home, and then later forget about as they get pushed to the back of the liquor cabinet.

In contrast, the liqueurs from Thomas & Sons are truly distinctive. They are often made with organic ingredients whenever possible and feature distinct flavor combinations that capture the subtlety of the teas and botanicals used. You'll be hooked. For example, Tea Spirit No. 16 - Spice Tea is made with a Yunnan black tea base and an infusion of ginger root, cassia, cinnamon, sweet orange peel, Curaçao peel, bergamot, and allspice.

AN ACQUIRED TASTE

ginger

Fernet-Branca, a brand of bitter liqueur from the Amaro family, is often referred to as "The Bartender's Handshake."

Cocktail bartenders in cities like San Francisco, New York, and Portland formed an unofficial "acquired taste club," while sipping on this unusual bitter liqueur together after shifts, and there's been somewhat of a cult following ever since.

Thomas & Sons released its own Northwest-style fernet, the Pacific Northwest Fernet, made with ingredients like Douglas fir, birch bark, and hops. Unlike the Fernet-Branca, it's less of an acquired taste and more approachable.

While adding tea to a cocktail isn't uncommon, the market for tea-based liqueurs is small. Very small, in fact. There's Tatratea, a tea-based herbal liqueur, produced by Karloff, based in the Slovak Republic. Other than that, it's difficult to name a tea-based liqueur that the average drinker would recognize. In that sense, Thomas & Sons is creating a truly authentic and novel product right here in Portland.

TASTING TIPS: GETTING THE MOST OUT OF YOUR VISIT

At Thomas & Sons Distillery, you'll find a seemingly covert tasting room located mere feet away from the equipment and production area where the kombucha is brewed and the spirits are distilled. As you enter this somewhat hidden tasting room, note the speakeasy vibe.

Tucked away behind a wall, the dimly lit, sumptuous bar is hidden so well that the distillers could have gotten away with not telling the Oregon Liquor Control Commission it even exists. The rich green paint on the walls, shiny display shelves

TEAHOUSE MASCOT

When Townshend's Tea Company commissioned artwork for its Alberta Street teahouse location, its sloth mascot was inadvertently created. (This was years before creatures like llamas, owls, and foxes became popular Portland spirit animals.) Otis the sloth has appeared all over the company's branding materials, gracing the labels on bottles and the framed prints hanging on the walls.

of bottled products, and opulent bar make this tasting room a glamorous gem among the tasting rooms in Portland.

Depending on the time of your visit, you might be able hear the hum of the production facility or the clanking of bottles on a Brew Dr. bottling day from the other side of the wall as you sip your tasting cups. If it's production or bottling time, you may need to speak up to be heard.

Thomas & Sons liqueurs are remarkable in cocktails. Try them all during your visit. Pick up some bottles of kombucha for the road or the next morning. Your gut may thank you after a day of tasting and a night of cocktails and bar snacks, which Thomas & Sons offers in smaller flights with less alcohol right there in the tasting room.

◆ Townshend's Tasting Menu ◆

Amaro: Kashmiri Amaro, Pacific Northwest Fernet

Gin: Townshend's Gin

Liqueur: Bluebird Alpine Liqueur

Tea-based spirit: Tea Spirit No. 2 - Sweet Tea, Tea Spirit No. 5 - Smoke Tea, Tea Spirit No. 16 - Spice Tea, Tea Spirit No. 50 - Bitter Tea, White Rose

High-Proof pick: For something you've likely never experienced, try the Bluebird Alpine Liqueur and enjoy this gently sweet liqueur all by itself to better appreciate the aromatic herbs and spices like angelica and fennel. For a subtle floral spirit, try the Townshend's White Rose made with white tea and rose petals. It's sippable on its own but also works great in complex cocktails.

Vinn Distillery

TASTING ROOM:
222 SE 8th Avenue • (503) 807-3826
Thursday–Friday, 1pm–4pm
Saturday, 12 noon–5 pm
Sunday, 1pm–5pm
www.vinndistillery.com

At a glance—→ Unique spirits made from rice, not found elsewhere in the U.S.

Founded by—→ Phan Ly.

What's in a name?—→ Five siblings in this distilling family share the same middle name, Vinn.

Tasting room vibes—→ Modern, elegant, and roomy.

Year opened—→ 2009.

Tours—→ None at the tasting room; distillery operations are located in Wilsonville, Oregon.

How to know you've arrived—→ You'll find yourself surrounded by larger warehouses and just a few restaurants sprinkled throughout the streets.

86'D FROM THE FAMILY RESTAURANT

Before they got into the business of distilling, the Ly family ran a restaurant in Wilsonville, Oregon called Wok Inn. The stress and backbreaking work of running a restaurant for twenty years inevitably took its toll on the founder of Vinn Distillery and father of the Ly family, Phan Ly. In a kind of intervention to deal with Phan's deteriorating health, the Ly children basically had to eighty-six their own father out of the business.

Begrudgingly, the father acquiesced. He didn't go into his "forced" retirement lightly. Phan began working on another project: distilling baijiu for legal sale (he had already been making baijiu for years for friends and family). It only made sense that Ly Senior would find another way to turn a profit on his ingenuity once again.

With extra time on his hands, Phan met up with his cousin living in Seattle who had worked for a French distillery in Vietnam. Phan knew he'd need to produce more than just baijiu to have a successful business plan. With the help of his cousin, he learned to make rice wine and added two rice wine products—Mijiu Fire and Mijiu Ice—to the original portfolio alongside rice-based baijiu.

A LONG JOURNEY TO OREGON

Before opening and operating a restaurant in Wilsonville, four generations of the Ly family migrated and settled in Quang Ninh Province in North Vietnam, just south of China's borders, seeking a better life. In 1978, the family was forced to leave and return to China. When the opportunity arose in the spring of 1979, Ly Senior found a ship and sailed it all the way to Hong Kong (under the British at the time), toting his family with him and nearly seventy other people too. Eventually, Meridian United Church of Christ arranged for the Ly family to emigrate to the U.S. They soon arrived in Oregon, settling down in the Portland suburb of Wilsonville.

In their new home, the Ly family members opened the restaurant, which Phan ran until his forced retirement two decades later. In his leisure years, Phan may have been banned from the restaurant's kitchen, but he still managed to sneak in every so often. When he needed rice for his baijiu recipe, he would plunder the restaurant's kitchen for supplies and rice cookers. To this day, those same 'looted' rice cookers are still in use at the distillery location in Wilsonville, cooking the rice used in Vinn spirits.

THE WORLD'S MOST CONSUMED LIQUOR

Chances are you've probably never heard of China's most popular alcohol called baijiu (pronounced BYE-joe), a spirit that has been produced and consumed by millions for somewhere between three to five thousand years or so, and is the world's largest spirit category today based on gross sales. Depending on the region, baijiu is distilled from sorghum (a grassy plant) or a cereal grain, such as rice, wheat, or corn. This very strong liquor tastes somewhat like an amalgamation of tequila, sake, and white rum. Strong in proof, baijiu clocks in at somewhere between 80 ABV and 120 ABV. It's usually served neat and consumed at meals.

THE POPULAR SPIRIT YOU'VE NEVER TRIED

Also known as "Fire Water," baijiu is a clear spirit made from one or more of these ingredients: sorghum, wheat, rice, sticky rice, and/or corn.

The style of baijiu the Ly family makes is from the southern region of China where the family is originally from. Distilled from brown rice and aged for one year, Vinn Baijiu is saké-like but has a heavier mouthfeel. There are hints of nuts, pepper, bark, and floral sweetness. Although the Vinn family has been distilling for generations, the baijiu they make at their distillery here is modified slightly to appeal to the American palate.

Basically, its potency is dialed down so that it's not quite jet fuel-grade. Most baijiu produced outside of the U.S. is 100 to 110 proof (hence, the nickname "Fire Water"). The baijiu that Vinn produces is a bit less, around 80 proof for accessibility to the local market.

TASTING TIPS: GETTING THE MOST OUT OF YOUR VISIT

Vinn Distillery's elegant and spacious tasting room makes this family-owned establishment the perfect place to bring a good-size group. You can rent the space for your next event or party for groups of up to thirty people. The wrap-around bar inside is roomy enough for a crowd, but it's comfortable enough, too, for an intimate soiree with friends or even a friendly one-on-one chat with the tasting room employees.

During a tasting, you can try all four Vinn spirits: the baijiu, vodka, whiskey, and blackberry liqueur. The tasting also includes two mini cocktails that rotate seasonally.

After you finish the tasting, check out the various goods, glassware, and barware it sells.

◆ Tasting Menu ◆

Baijiu (**a.k.a. fire water**): Vinn Baijiu

Vodka: Vinn Blackberry Liqueur (Vinn Vodka infused with blackberries), Vinn Vodka

Whiskey: Vinn Whiskey

High-Proof pick: If you had to choose only one, go for the Vinn Baijiu. Baijiu translates to "white liquor," though its potency earns it its other monikers, "White Devil" and "Fire Water." This baijiu packs a punch, but once you've had your first buzz, you'll be reaching for more, as well as convincing friends to give it a try. Get traditional and drink it along with a meal, or try your hand at mixing this potent spirit in your cocktails at home.

For another novelty, try the Vinn Vodka, the first rice vodka produced and bottled in the U.S. Made from a family recipe passed down through seven generations, this vodka is smooth, creamy, and clean, with a slightly sweet finish that you don't usually get in traditional formulas. Like the vodka, the Vinn Whiskey is also the only one of its kind produced and bottled domestically. Aged in oak barrels, Vinn Whiskey offers a palate-pleasing, malty, creamy taste.

WILD ROOTS VODKA

TASTING ROOM:
135 NE 6th Avenue • (974) 254-4617

Thursday–Sunday, 12 noon–5pm

TASTING ROOM & DISTILLERY:
575 East Sun Ranch Drive
Sisters, OR 97759

www.wildrootsvodka.com

At a glance⟶ Vodka infused with fruit from the Pacific Northwest.

Founded by⟶ Chris Joseph

What's in a name?⟶ Inspired by the native regional fruit used in the vodka and Chris Joseph's own "roots" in the Portland area.

Tasting room vibes⟶ A light-filled space with a modern industrial feel.

Year opened⟶ Vodka hit the shelves in 2013; the tasting room opened in 2014.

Tours⟶ None.

How to know you've arrived⟶ One block over on E Burnside Street, you'll see newly built condos and older buildings that house hip pizza joints, boutiques, nightclubs, and dive bars.

DEEP OREGON ROOTS

In Portland, where the all-natural, local, and handmade mantra reigns supreme, many food and drink purveyors establish their footing by experimenting with native produce, fruit, and plant life in their products. It was no different for Oregon-born Chris Joseph, who founded Northwest Natural Spirits (NWNS) in 2012. A year later, NWNS evolved to become Wild Roots Vodka, with a new focus on fruit infusions.

WILD ABOUT VODKA INFUSIONS: PUSHING THE BOUNDARIES OF DISTILLERY ROW

While Wild Roots Vodka has a Northeast Portland address, it's actually very close to E Burnside Street, the unofficial boundary between Southeast and Northeast Portland.

Wild Roots may have rooted itself on NE 6th Avenue, technically outside of Southeast Portland, but it has been a proud member of the Distillery Row family ever since it started. At the time, Northwest Natural Spirits sensed a vacuum—and an opportunity. "There were no natural options. Artificial fruit extracts, flavors, and colors lined the shelves, and we knew something had to be done." To Chris, it only made sense to produce their vodka infusions on a much grander scale.

Soon the kitchen was too small for their vision, and Chris moved operations to his father's garage. Wild Roots started its bottling operation as a private label using the Bendistillery distillate, before it moved on to bottling its own stuff in a facility in Hillsboro, just twenty miles west of Portland.

By 2013, bottles of Wild Roots Vodka were sitting on liquor store shelves and stocked at local bars. A year later, Wild Roots opened its first tasting room at its current location on NE 6th Avenue.

INFUSED VODKA VS. LIQUEURS

Both infused vodka and fruit liqueurs have a fruit base, but the difference lies in the processes used when they're made. With infused vodka, fruit is added to the base liquor, which infuses the spirit. Wild Roots uses about a pound of fruit in the production of each bottle. With liqueur, the fruit itself is fermented to produce the distillate.

They also differ in potency. Liqueur tends to be lower in alcohol than infused vodka. Wild Roots vodka is rich in flavor and sits on the shelf with a potency of 70-80 proof, whereas you'll find plenty of liqueur hovering around 40 proof.

TASTING TIPS: GETTING THE MOST OUT OF YOUR VISIT

When you first visit the tasting room at Wild Roots Vodka, you'll notice how the contemporary, industrial feel evokes a modern condominium architectural aesthetic: cement floors, panels of big windows, and high ceilings. With large groups, the space can get very crowded, but it feels spacious enough to keep a small party happy and comfortable.

Wild Roots's bar is equipped to serve small taster cups and mini cocktails. The mini cocktails change with the season and highlight how flavorful infused vodka is as a base in mixed drinks.

◆ Tasting Menu ◆

Vodka: Northwest Organic Vodka, Northwest Red Raspberry Vodka, Oregon Marionberry Vodka, Washington Apple & Cinnamon Vodka, Northwest Pear Vodka, Northwest Cranberry Vodka, Sweet Cherry Vodka

Note: Every bottle contains a pound of real berries or fruit all sourced from Pacific Northwest farms.

High-Proof pick: Oregon Marionberry Vodka is bold in flavor and mouthfeel, but not so bold that you have to mix it in a complicated cocktail to enjoy it. I have a friend who routinely drinks the Marionberry Vodka over ice with a bit of lemon. As a summer drink, it's simple, easy, and perfect.

NW DISTILLERIES

BULL RUN DISTILLING
COMPANY

CLEAR CREEK DISTILLERY

MARTIN RYAN DISTILLING
(ARIA GIN)

BULL RUN DISTILLING COMPANY

TASTING ROOM & DISTILLERY:
2259 NW Quimby St. ◆ (503) 224-3483
Wednesday–Sunday, 12 noon–6pm
www.bullrundistillery.com

At a glance—→ A whiskey-heavy portfolio with regional Pacific Northwest qualities and flavors.

Founded by—→ Lee Medoff (Lee was previously co-owner of House Spirits Distillery), and whiskey-loving college friends Patrick Bernards, John Rudi, and Michael Maher.

What's in a name?—→ A nod to the water from the Bull Run Watershed used by the distillery, and a reference to the ranchers in the 1850s who crossed the Cascade Mountains with cattle. Also, a tongue-in-cheek play on whiskey's masculine virility.

Tasting room vibes—→ Small and cozy. It's the perfect spot for drinkers serious about their tasters.

Year opened—→ 2010

Tours—→ By chance. While there, ask and you may receive. Group tours are available by appointment. Call ahead to schedule.

How to know you've arrived—→ The immediate area around Bull Run is filled with industrial warehouses and the hustle and bustle of NW 23rd Avenue, with its shops, restaurants, and bars.

DRINKING UP IDEAS

Have you ever come up with a great plan while drinking? I'm not talking about a random thought like jumping into a swimming pool or going to the rooftop of your building to watch the sunset. I'm talking about a "let's talk real business, right here, over this drink" kind of scheming.

It happened this way for Bull Run Distilling founders in 2010 over drinks at Skyline Tavern, a bar on top of Tualatin Mountain, one thousand and sixty feet in elevation, with scenic views of Portland's Forest Park. The plan was hatched to put Oregon-made whiskey on the map. Later, as the business evolved, Lee would focus on developing a portfolio laden with whiskey made from their signature Oregon Single Malt—to merchant bottling expressions with unique barrel finishes. Patrick would focus on the business side of running the distillery, until he parted ways with Bull Run Distilling Company in 2015.

A PAST IN SPIRITS: BULL RUN'S STILL LIFE

Bull Run's twin eight hundred gallon pot stills are among the largest used by craft distillers in Portland and were custom-designed and built locally in Portland, Oregon. When you visit the Bull Run tasting room, ask for a tour. Chances are someone will be able to show you the impressive hardware that produces Bull Run's spirits.

While Lee doesn't have a bone to pick with gin, he had a desire to produce a more whiskey-heavy line-up. At Bull Run, he shifted his concentration from the juniper berries and other botanicals of gin making to the malted barley of whiskey production. When Lee left House Spirits and started Bull Run, he brought Medoyeff Vodka with him, reclaiming the family's original spelling and a tribute to his Russian grandfather who settled in Portland after the Russian Revolution.

Lee's background in alcohol production in Oregon began at as a brewer for McMenamins. Next he had a stint working in a winery in France, where he had his first encounter with distilling. After learning to master a small alembic still making fiery marc (French for pomace) he returned to Oregon. From there, Lee went on to return to McMenamins, where he met Christian Krogstad, his future partner at House Spirits Distillery.

It was a being-in-the-right-place-at-the-right-time kind of situation that jumpstarted Lee's career in distilling. He was a brewer for McMenamins when the company decided to expand its product line to include spirits. McMenamins Edgefield was erected in 1998, and it was there where Lee began experimenting. He used his background in winemaking and brewing to help McMenamins create the system it has in place today.

The experience influenced Lee's profession immensely. He was sold on distilling. "In distilling, you put beer and wine into a still, you get something new and different. Unlike with winemaking, the connection [to the source of the ingredients] isn't as obvious."

Lee was intrigued by barrel finishing and blending early on. The ability to change the makeup of a spirit based on the environment (for example, the kind of barrel where a whiskey is stored) inspired him. This kind of love for exploring and concocting flavors drives the whiskey production at Bull Run to this day.

THE FORMULA FOR SUCCESS

They say good pizza crust is about the water used in the dough. Breweries will tell you the same thing: good beer is definitely about the water that goes in, as much as it is about the grains and hops. In the same way, Bull Run honors the "it's the water" philosophy by using only the pristine waters that run through the Bull Run Watershed in its distilling process. Using the naturally soft water from Bull Run Watershed contributes to the mouthfeel of Bull Run spirits.

Aside from the water, Bull Run values the ingredients used in its whiskey, particularly the malted barley. Malted barley is prevalent in Oregon, which means the whiskey at Bull Run reflects a regional style that you'd be hard-pressed to find anywhere else.

PORTLAND'S (FORMER) UNDERBELLY

Many people don't know that the area of Northwest Portland where Bull Run Distilling makes its home boasts a rather sordid past. Long before NW 23rd Avenue was referred to as "Trendy-Third," it was known as "Slabtown," an area grittier, rowdier, and grungier than today's polished version.[1] Instead of elegant boutiques, craft cocktail bars, luxurious lingerie stores, and artisan ice cream shops lining the streets, there were shady brothels, crowded boarding houses, and boisterous saloons. Amid the sawmills that formed the city's first major industry, a general sense of lawlessness pervaded. Underneath the economic progress, urban blight lurked.

The name Slabtown refers to the offcuts or "slabs" of wood leftover by the lumber mills in the area. The growing population of working poor who lived in the crowded work camps and tenements around the mills burned these pieces of wood for fuel and heating. The mills and workers eventually moved away as the timber industry in Portland changed, but the name Slabtown persisted.

As you'll notice when you visit Bull Run Distilling's

---

[1] From "Portland's Slabtown" (Arcadia Publishing, 2013) by Mike Ryerson, Norm Gholston, and Tracy J. Prince

Northwest Portland tasting room, the area it calls home is no longer the dark urban underbelly it used to be. Most, if any, of the boisterous behavior you'll observe today comes in the form of unruly children on play dates.

TASTING TIPS: GETTING THE MOST OUT OF YOUR VISIT

Bull Run Distilling doesn't want to be just another obligatory stop on your spirits crawl. If you come by for a tour, take your time and get to know the company's intriguing whiskey line-up.

Bull Run Distilling likes to mix it up in creative ways, and this shines through in its products. For example, while the standard method for making whiskey is to use only new charred barrels, Bull Run works with local coopers to fashion barrels from unconventional wood like cherry, apple, and Oregon juniper as well as sourcing used barrels from the local wine and brewing industries. The Temperance Trader Chinato Barrel Aged Bourbon, for example, also uses sweet vermouth barrels sourced from Cana's Feast Winery in Carlton, Oregon, during part of the aging process. The used wine barrels impart rich flavor notes like oak, prunes, and vanilla spice.

Bull Run's tasting room is on the smaller side but is likely to expand. Larger groups can be accommodated, though groups smaller than five will be the most comfortable.

◆ Tasting Menu ◆

Aquavit: Regnig Dag Aquavit

Rum: Pacific Rum (distilled from Hawaiian Turbinado Sugar)

Vodka: Medoyeff Starka (barrel-aged in pinot noir barrels), Medoyeff Vodka (full-grain, European-style)

Whiskey: Oregon Single Malt Whiskey, Oregon Single

Malt Whiskey - Cask Strength, American Whiskey, Straight Bourbon Whiskey, Straight Bourbon Whiskey - Barrel Strength, Chinato

High-Proof pick: Don't pass up the chance to try the Chinato Barrel Aged Bourbon. It's an innovation happening in whiskey-making that you shouldn't miss: a bourbon aged and finished in both old vermouth barrels and the usual new, charred oak barrels. You'll taste hints of oak, wine, and some vanilla and caramel in this soft-drinking whiskey. Introduce your palate to what's on the horizon: Oregon-made whiskey as its own category. Try Bull Run's Oregon Single Malt Whiskey for a taste of this well-done burgeoning category.

CLEAR CREEK DISTILLERY

TASTING ROOM & DISTILLERY:
2389 NW Wilson St. • (503)248-9470
Sunday–Friday, 12 noon–6pm;
Saturday, 10am–6pm
For tastings outside regular hours,
e-mail info@clearcreekdistillery.com

www.clearcreekdistillery.com

At a glance⟶ The grandfather of distilling in Oregon, producing eau de vie, grappa, and a variety of liqueurs.

Founded by⟶ Steve McCarthy

What's in a name?⟶ Named for the river that runs through the McCarthy family orchards. It also describes the clear brandy they make.

Tasting room vibes⟶ A warm and inviting space with enough room for a small group to move around in and mingle.

Year opened⟶ 1985. It's the oldest operating distillery in Portland.

Tours⟶ On Saturdays at 2pm and 4pm.

How to know you've arrived⟶ Clear Creek is accessible off of Interstate 405 and close to the hustle and bustle on NW 23rd Avenue. It's also seemingly off-the-beaten-path, tucked away in an area in Northwest Portland surrounded by nondescript warehouses and machine shops.

BRINGING EUROPE BACK TO OREGON

After traveling through France, the Swiss Alps, and other parts of Europe in the late 1970s and 1980s, Steve McCarthy returned to Oregon with the desire to replicate the bone-dry, fruit spirits he drank while traveling the region. Fortunately, he only had to look to his own family's backyard in Parkdale, Oregon, for inspiration.

Steve's family has owned orchards in Oregon for decades, going as far back as the early twentieth century. The family was one of the first to settle in the Hood River Valley back in the day. During the Great Depression, the family lost the orchards, though later was able to buy them back.

Steeped in these traditions and practices, and still reeling from his experience with European liqueurs, Steve began to look at the orchard harvests in new ways. With the ingredients for grappa, eau de vie, and brandy so readily accessible, Steve began learning everything he could about the distillation process. The goal: to use local bounty with European techniques.

Steve quickly threw himself into study mode, researching the art of distilling any way he could. (This was long before Google was even a noun, let alone a verb.) He reached out to the few people in California who were distilling these spirits for advice. He asked questions, collected tips, and sketched out ideas. From there, it was months and months of relentless trial-and-error to perfect a portfolio of spirits that was not only exotic to the Pacific Northwest but also borne from it.

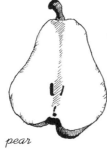

pear

THE MYSTERIOUS PEAR-IN-BOTTLE

One of Clear Creek Distillery's most recognizable spirits is its pear-in-the-bottle pear brandy. It might remind you of mezcal and its ubiquitous worm. Where the worm in mezcal is added at the end of the process, the pear in this brandy lives and grows from inside of the bottle from the very beginning. Going from the fruit bud to bottle is Clear Creek's stamp, inspired by the same practices Steve observed while he spent time in France during his youth.

Getting the pear inside the glass bottle is more arduous than simply dropping worm larvae down the porthole of a bottle, as is done with mezcal. The process starts long before the pears are even harvested, around the time the tree has begun to bud in the spring. A clear glass bottle is slipped over the tiny bud and delicately tied to the tree with twine. The bottle stays on the branch through the summer while the pear grows inside, lovingly tended by hand. Once the pear has matured to average size inside its miniature greenhouse, usually by late summer, the pear-in-bottles are then harvested. Because the bottles are exposed to the elements, the bottles are then meticulously scrubbed, again by hand, before the brandy is finally added.

CHANGING LOCATION AND HANDS

Clear Creek Distillery's first location was on NW 23rd Avenue and NW Quimby Street, in the building that is now The Matador. The previous tenant of Clear Creek's current Wilson Street building came by Clear Creek one day to buy some products and told the distillers he was moving from the Wilson warehouse to a bigger space. The distillers jumped at the opportunity for more production space. When they moved to the Wilson Street location, they bought over two more stills, ultimately doubling production.

In 2014, Hood River Distillers, known for Pendleton Whisky, acquired Clear Creek Distillery. Clear Creek Distillery's extensive product list still boasts an extensive brandy, whiskey and grappa production.

TASTING TIPS: GETTING THE MOST OUT OF YOUR VISIT

There is a limit of five tasters per visitor per day for a small tasting fee. Grab a tasting menu and choose up to five from any category. Keep track of the spirits you've already tasted. If you're serious about getting to know Clear Creek Distillery's menu, I recommend starting with a few brandies and returning another day to sample the other spirits. From the brandy collection, definitely save the Douglas Fir Brandy for the end since it will leave a lingering taste in your mouth and affect your palate.

◆ Tasting Menu ◆

Clear Brandy (Eau de Vie): Pear, Pear in the Bottle, Cherry, Blue Plum, Mirabelle Plum, Raspberry, Douglas Fir

Barrel Aged Brandy: Apple Reserve, Apple, American Pot Still

Liqueurs: Cranberry, Marionberry, Loganberry, Cassis, Cherry, Raspberry, Pear

Grappa: Muscat, Pinot Noir, Nebbiolo, Sangiovese

Whiskey: McCarthy's Oregon Single Malt Whiskey

High-Proof pick: Try the Pear Brandy as a gateway spirit to understanding what good brandy should taste like. For another rare delight, go for the Douglas Fir Eau de Vie. Inspired by the Alsatian Eau de Vie de Bourgeons de Sapin, Clear Creek developed an iconic Pacific Northwest version. Douglas fir buds are gathered by hand and added to a clear brandy, which is then later re-distilled and re-infused for even woodsier flavor.

Martin Ryan Distilling Company

---•---

TASTING ROOM & DISTILLERY:
2304 NW Savier St.
Wednesday–Sunday, 12 noon–6pm
sayhello@ariagin.com
www.ariagin.com

At a glance—→ Superlative English-inspired Portland dry gin.

Founded by—→ Erik Martin and Ryan Csanky

What's in a name?—→ A combination of the last name and first name of the founders.

Tasting room vibes—→ Art gallery sensibility featuring decorative displays of gin ingredients and barwares.

Year opened—→ Started distilling in 2012; the tasting room opened in 2015.

Tours—→ Available upon request.

How to know you've arrived—→ You'll find yourself dodging moms in yoga gear pushing strollers, and then weaving around couples strolling down the sidewalk on the way to get ice cream, before reaching the classy exterior of this former antiques store turned art gallery-inspired tasting room.

GROWN-UP GIN

If you told me you didn't like flavored fortified wines (think: Night Train Express or maybe even Mad Dog), I wouldn't judge you. If you had only given gin a good college try and turned your back since then, I'd tell you that you were missing out big time and I might judge you slightly.

It's very likely that you don't like gin because there was a lot of inferior gin out there that made for a bad first impression. It's also likely you just haven't found the right gin to please your palate. If you're a gin lover who has tried to convert an adamant gin hater, you know the skeptical look you get from those who haven't tried enough gin to find the one they love. Trust me, if you find the right high-quality gin, you might find yourself drinking gin like the statesman or soldier who shared a fondness for the liquor in its long storied history.

HOW MARTIN RYAN DOES GIN: A BRAND IS BORN

"Aria" is an Italian word, a musical term referring to works with an expressive melody performed by a solo singer. Ryan noticed the word when flipping through a magazine. It sounded elegant and fit in with Erik's love for music (Erik was a bassist in a band at the time).

While sitting at Paymaster Lounge, then called Balls the Cat's Moonshine Kitchen & Lounge, in the Slabtown neighborhood, Ryan sketched out his ideas for Aria's logo on a cocktail napkin. He liked the idea of a hand-written, recognizable logo that was more artistic than straightforward. From there, Ryan designed the rest of the bottle, the website, and all other marketing materials.

Aria Portland Dry Gin is made with ten classic gin botanicals: angelica root, cardamom, cassia bark, coriander, cubeb berry, lemon peel, grains of paradise, juniper, orange peel, and orris root. For the truly curious, all these ingredients are available to touch and smell in the Aria tasting room.

THE ROAD TO ARIA

Founders Erik Martin and Ryan Csanky have been toasting "Prost!" to one another since their tenth grade German language class where they first met. After graduating from Sunset High School in Beaverton, Oregon, the two stayed around the Portland area and started Artisan Spirits with partner Shane Thatcher in 2007. Artisan Spirits shut its doors in 2010. Ryan had been tending bar at the Wildwood Restaurant, a farm-to-table Portland institution that had been around for twenty years. (It later closed in 2014.) Meanwhile, Erik continued his career in paralegal work, which would eventually become helpful in understanding the legalese of starting a distillery business.

By 2012, Erik and Ryan were back to their old ways, and together they started Martin Ryan Distilling Company. They realized that their love for creating exceptional spirits hadn't dissipated. Still holding down their full-time jobs, Erik and Ryan began producing Aria Portland Dry Gin at Bull Run Distilling Company. They had a three-year run of production there, until they moved on to running their own tasting room and distillery in November 2015.

FROM ANTIQUE STORE TO GIN GALLERY

For nearly two years, the two founders held down full-time jobs while making award-winning Aria Portland Dry Gin. Ryan was walking home from breakfast

SHAKEN, NOT STIRRED

You've heard the oft-used James Bond quote, "shaken, not stirred." It's been said that this very quote ruined the martini. Shaking a martini adds bubbles to the liquid, which creates a murky, cloudy cocktail.

GIN 101

School your palate. Before you head to Martin Ryan Distilling for its Aria Portland Dry Gin, learn the different styles of gin and their different tasting notes:

- London Dry Gin: The most recognizable gin out there. Well-known brands include Tanqueray, Bombay Sapphire, and Beefeater.

- Modern, Contemporary, or New Western: Defined by the use of nontraditional ingredients. Juniper often plays less of a role in the flavor profile.

- Old Tom Gin: Popular back in the 1800s and early 1900s, Old Tom Gin is now making a comeback. A bit sweeter than London Dry Gin, Old Tom Gin is primarily found in Tom Collins and Ramos Gin Fizz cocktails.

- Plymouth Gin: Made in Plymouth, England, this type of gin is drier in taste than London Dry Gin and has softer juniper notes. Try this if you never liked Tanqueray.

in the neighborhood when he passed the current 23rd Avenue location. At the time it was home to Jerry Lamb Interiors & Antiques. Ryan noticed the moving sale sign hanging in one of the store windows and got a hold of the building's landlord. He found out the space would be listed for rent that year. It was an easy deal to seal. The landlord told Ryan he wanted to see a distillery or a brewery go into the space.

Martin Ryan eventually remodeled the building and transformed it from an antiques store to the new home of Aria Portland Dry Gin, turning it into the "gallery" of Portland drinking it is today.

WHY JUST GIN?

Were you wondering, why only gin? Part of the answer to this is rooted in what we know about distilling in general.

For most distilleries, gin is just a quick stop along the way. Distilleries everywhere, even outside of Portland, often start out making vodka because it's cheaper and faster to produce with no aging time, and then move on to gin, and then eventually move on to making whiskey. Sadly, gin is often treated like the middle child in the family—ignored—while vodka and whiskey get all of the distiller's attention. When Martin Ryan began distilling Aria, the distillers saw that no one in Portland was producing dry gin with a robust focus.

The product's quality speaks for itself. Eventually, the distillers may try aging gin in different barrels or making other flavored one-offs. As of now, Martin Ryan's concentration will be primarily English-style dry gin.

The good news is that gin is a must-have for many classic cocktails. It's an exceptional base for recreating old school libations like a Gin Rickey or Bee's Knees. Gin has been used in mixology for hundreds of years, but it's also a favorite for new, cutting-edge drinks. According to Ryan, the mix of botanicals in gin makes it super receptive to the person mixing the cocktail. Different bartenders might play off of the different botanicals in the gin when mixing more complex, creative cocktails. This makes gin much more versatile than other spirits, such as vodka.

TASTING TIPS: GETTING THE MOST OUT OF YOUR VISIT

If you love gin, I have news for you: Martin Ryan's tasting room is completely devoted to its top-selling Aria Portland Dry Gin. It's remarkable in cocktails—both classics and new ones. Try the distillery's rotating series of seasonal cocktails made with some of the local bitters, syrups, and tonics that are sold in the tasting room. A flight tasting starts with the gin on its own, followed by four sample sized (½ oz. only—no full drinks) cocktails that change roughly every month. Recipes are always on the website, so you can easily recreate them at home.

Even if you don't like gin, give it a try. Also, don't forget to peruse the Aria retail store for all of the ingredients and barware to make a great gin cocktail, such as a Bull in China mixing glass or stirred drink set.

Martin Ryan's tasting room is part of the NW Distiller's District. Martin Ryan, Bull Run Distilling Company, and Clear Creek Distillery are all within walking distance of one another (about six or seven blocks, or less than a mile apart). This means you could easily avoid driving by taking public transportation or walking.

◆ Tasting Menu ◆

Gin: Aria Portland Dry Gin

High-Proof pick: Don't miss the four sample sized cocktails that change roughly every month.

ROAD TRIP

INDUSTRIAL ROW DISTILLERY
(DYSTOPIA VODKA)

CRAFT SPIRITS
OUTSIDE OF PORTLAND

INDUSTRIAL ROW DISTILLERY
(DYSTOPIA VODKA)

TASTING ROOM & DISTILLERY:
645 N Tillamook St. • (503) 893-4730

Saturday, 1pm–5pm

www.irdistillery.com
www.dystopiavodka.com

At a glance—→ Unfiltered vodka with a singular, uncompromising vision.

Founded by—→ Nelson D'Amour.

What's in a name?—→ A nod to the founder's love for dystopian literature.

Tasting room vibes—→ Artsy drinking parlor filled with curated books and furniture in North Portland. To some, North is a road trip.

Year opened—→ 2011

Tours—→ Available by appointment.

How to know you've arrived—→ You'll be surrounded by rows of 1930s era warehouses, some of which used to have back doors that opened directly onto the railroad lines.

DYSTOPIAN STORIES

In the 1950s, science fiction legend Ray Bradbury wrote a short story called "The Veldt" about a family who lives in an automated house called 'The Happylife Home.' Technology in the home does everything for the family, from cooking meals, cleaning up, dressing everyone, and taking care of the children with a kind of virtual reality nursery. Eventually, all this convenience is revealed to have a dark side with dangerous repercussions for the family. It's the kind of story you read and never forget. It was one I never forgot after reading it for the first time in the sixth grade.

Nelson D'Amour loves this kind of dystopian literature for the way it turns a critical eye on society and contemporary social ills—and it's one of the reasons he came up with the label name, Dystopia Vodka.

On the Industrial Row website, Nelson writes:

" …[D]ystopia stands as a counterpoint to this [dishonest marketing practices] by exposing the truth about how other 'handcrafted' spirits are made and how ours differs—actually handmade, mashed, fermented, distilled, and bottled in the same 90-year-old former grain mill."

He has two undergraduate degrees, one in physics and the other in chemical engineering, from Columbia University, and a doctorate in chemical engineering from Stanford University. One night, while drinking in a bar, Nelson had a revelation and decided he wanted to distill vodka. At this time, he worked in technology development at Intel. Going from the tech world to the craft spirits scene became the perfect intersection of art, science, and business for Nelson, allowing him to bring together his far-ranging interests in spirits, engineering, cooking, graphic design, marketing, and interior remodeling.

BACKED BY VISION

Nelson is a one-man force of nature at Industrial Row Distillery. He designs all of Dystopia's branding, packaging, and labels. The interiors of the tasting room have Nelson's aesthetic touches. A print of Shepard Fairey's "Evolve Devolve," with its scene of an oil pump and windmill set against a burning sky, graces the wall. Look around the tasting room a little more and find recipe books with note pages labeled "hopes," "dreams," and "propaganda," as well as T-shirts and other merchandise promoting the Industrial Row vision.

Nelson has also used the distillery to bring together musicians and artists for shows and exhibitions, and has even recorded an exclusive album for the brand called Dystopian Dreams (download the album for free at www.dystopiavodka.com/#culture). There's also more space in the back of the distillery for live shows and performances.

MORE FLAVOR, LESS BURN

What's the main difference between most vodkas? The filtration; or, rather, when filtration happens in the process. For Nelson, filtering means you want to remove something that's unwanted. Nelson filters the water at the start of the distilling process, not the resulting distillate. The logic goes: if filtration takes place early on, then there's no need to filter the distillate afterwards.

The outcome is an unfiltered vodka that packs a lot of flavor with less burn. Dystopia is a grain-based vodka made with Bob's Red Mill organic grains. The water used in Dystopia is sourced from the Bull Run Watershed, Portland's pristine natural drinking water source used by many distillers and brewers. While many breweries and distillers use the water as-is because it's just that good, Nelson prefers to filter it using carbon filtration and reverse osmosis for an even purer, mineral-free H_2O.

Due to the water, there's a heavier, more robust mouthfeel setting it apart from mainstream vodka on the market.

Dystopia is smooth and creamy with floral tasting notes that reflect the rye and wheat grains used.

TASTING TIPS: GETTING THE MOST OUT OF YOUR VISIT

Industrial Row's tasting room is a classy and artsy drinking parlor filled with thoughtfully curated books and furniture, including a tufted leather couch. When you visit, plan to stay and hang out a bit. Through a window in the tasting room, you can get a glimpse of the in-house laboratory where the vodka was developed, though these days it's less about experimenting with new formulas and more about perfecting the existing one.

With its North Portland location, Industrial Row isn't conveniently located to the other distilleries in town, but just the same you can make a day of visiting its tasting room and drinking its fine spirit, alongside touring some of North Portland's best bars and restaurants. Your spirits exploration doesn't have to stop after your tasting tour at Industrial Row. Check out the offerings around North/Northeast Portland or head to the inner Industrial Southeast to check out more distilleries.

◆ Tasting Menu ◆

Vodka: Dystopia Vodka—the solo product at Industrial Row Distillery.

High-Proof pick: Try the vodka; it might just change your mind about sipping straight vodka. If you're not really a vodka drinker, you'll still appreciate this one because of the smoothness: there's less burn and less hints of ethanol. As a result, Dystopia Vodka is remarkably sippable compared to other vodka you might have tried before. Vodka on its own can have flavor, and Dystopia is packed with it. The taste of the grains comes through with floral notes.

CRAFT SPIRITS OUTSIDE OF PORTLAND

Distilleries right outside of the city have greatly contributed to the distilling scene in Portland. In fact, many of the city's craft spirit makers like Christian Krogstad of House Spirits Distillery and Lee Medoff of Bull Run Distilling Company got their start at McMenamins Edgefield in Troutdale, Oregon. Rogue Spirits, which has a branch in Newport on the Oregon coast, was the first distillery in the state to produce rum. Right outside of Tigard, half an hour away, Indio Spirits makes award-winning liquors found in many cocktail bars around Portland. (John Ufford formed Indio Spirits in Portland in 2004 before opening another tasting room in Portland in 2016.)

Though most of the products from the distilleries in this chapter can be found at Portland liquor stores, you'll do yourself a solid by hopping in your car and visiting these tasting rooms in person. Most places listed here are just a beautiful drive away in any direction. Who can say no to a road trip?

DRIVING TIMES FROM PORTLAND:

- About 30 minutes: Clackamas, Hillsboro, Tigard, Troutdale
- About 1 hour: McMinnville
- About 1½ hours: Cannon Beach, Hood River
- Under 2 hours: Eugene
- Under 3 hours: Newport
- Over 3 hours: Bend

Whether you're heading straight to the distillery or taking a trip to see some of Oregon's natural wonders, while soaking up the sun or taking in the mountain air, distilleries all over Oregon beckon with their welcoming tasting rooms. Gather your friends together and continue your high-proof "research" on the road.

BEND

BackDrop Distilling
70 SW Century Drive, Suites 100-298 ♦ (541) 728-0860
www.backdropdistilling.com
Call or e-mail cocktails@backdropdistilling.com to book
a private tour
Driving time from Portland: over 3 hours

BackDrop kept it simple by starting out with just vodka, rum, and gin production in 2015. This relatively new distillery is located inside of the GoodLife Brewing Company. When you sign up for a private tour, you'll see a German copper still used in the distilling process and sip spirits made with Tumalo Creek water.

- *Tasting Menu:* BackDrop Gin, BackDrop Rum, BackDrop Vodka

  High-Proof pick: The BackDrop Rum is made from a mix of dark and light rum aged in bourbon barrels.

Bendistillery (Crater Lake Spirits)
19330 Pinehurst Road (tasting room & distillery) ♦ (541) 318-0200
1024 NW Bond Street (tasting room only) ♦ (541) 480-3483
www.craterlakespirits.com
Monday–Saturday, 11am–5pm; Sunday, 11am–4pm
Driving time from Portland: over 3 hours

When Bendistillery started in 1996, it released gin and vodka, putting the distillery on the map as one of just a handful of distilleries in the state. In 2010, it expanded operations, moving to a twenty-four-acre farm property in Tumalo, Oregon. Try Crater Lake Spirits at the tasting room and distillery right off of Highway 20 or at the downtown tasting room on NW Bond Street near Deschutes Brewery & Public House. Crater Lake

Spirits are versatile; sip them alone or add them to cocktails.

Tasting Menu: gin (Crater Lake Estate Gin, Crater Lake Gin), vodka (Crater Lake Hatch Green Chile Vodka, Crater Lake Hazelnut Espresso Vodka, Crater Lake Pepper Vodka, Crater Lake Reserve Vodka, Crater Lake Sweet Ginger Vodka, Crater Lake Vodka), whiskey (Crater Lake Rye Whiskey)

High-Proof pick: For a taste of Oregon, go for the Crater Lake Gin. The gin's juniper berries are hand-picked from trees—some over a thousand years old—grown in the high desert of Central Oregon.

Cascade Alchemy
20585 Brinson Boulevard, Suite 5 ◆ (541) 647-4363
www.cascadealchemy.com
Monday–Saturday, 11am–3pm
Driving time from Portland: over 3 hours

Aside from meeting the distillers and seeing where your hooch is made, another reason to head to Cascade Alchemy's tasting room is to buy products that are unavailable at liquor stores. For example, the Barley Shine, made from locally-brewed beer, is only available for purchase in the distillery's retail store since it's produced in such small batches. Try the Barley Shine and other flavored spirits like the Apple Pie and Chai Tea Vodka.

Tasting Menu: gin (Oregon Gin, Aged Oregon Gin), vodka (Apple Pie, Barley Shine, Chai Tea Vodka, Hot Pepper Vodka, Vodka), whiskey (Bourbon)

High-Proof pick: The smooth aftertaste of the malted barely in the Barley Shine makes it a fine choice for something new and fresh.

Oregon Spirit Distillers

490 NE Butler Market Road ♦ (541) 382-0002
www.oregonspiritdistillers.com
Daily, 12 noon–7pm
Tours: Mon–Fri at 5pm; Sat–Sun at 2pm & 5pm
Driving time from Portland: over 3 hours

Oregon Spirit Distillers is best known for its bourbon, vodka, and genever gin production. After an expansion in 2014 and 2015, it tripled in size and increased production. Along with bigger facilities, the distillery also added the Barrel Thief Lounge, its own cocktail bar, where patrons can order full-size cocktails made with Oregon Spirit Distillers craft spirits and eat bar snacks.

> *Tasting Menu:* absinthe (Wild Card Absinthe),
> gin (Merrylegs Genever, Scribbles Dry Gin), whis-
> key (C.W. Irwin Bourbon, J. Becher Rye Whiskey,
> Oregon, J. Becher Rye Whiskey Bottled in Bond,
> Oregon Spirit Bourbon, Oregon Spirit Bourbon
> Bottled in Bond, Oregon Spirit Wheat, Oregon Spirit
> Wheat Whiskey Bottled in Bond, Ottis Webber Wheat
> Whiskey)

> *High-Proof pick:* Go for the Ottis Webber Oregon
> Wheat Whiskey, one of Oregon's first wheat whiskeys
> made from high desert wheat and aged for three years
> in New American oak barrels.

Cannon Beach Distillery

255 N Hemlock Street ◆ (503) 436-0301
www.cannonbeachdistillery.com
Daily, 12 noon–6pm
Driving time from Portland: about 1½ hours

Oregon's crowd-pleasing Cannon Beach, known for its picturesque haystack rocks, may have hoards of tourists combing its sands, but Cannon Beach Distillery is still one discovery yet to be overturned by many. The company has three collections: the Rock Series, Tidal Series, and Carronade Collection. The Rock Series is made up of an agave spirit (not tequila; more similar to brandy) and two types of rum. The Tidal Series is mostly gin, and the Carronade Collection consists of small batches of mostly whiskey sold exclusively at the tasting room.

Tasting Menu: agave spirits (Il Keyote), gin (Lost Buoy Gin, Peters' Family Gin, Old Tom Gin), rum (Dorymen's Rum, Donlon Shanks Amber Rum, Spiced Rum), whiskey (Carronade Single-Release Series)

High-Proof pick: A rum made from blackstrap molasses, the Donlon Shanks Amber Rum has a deeper, more robust flavor than other types of rum. Definitely worth a try.

EUGENE

Crescendo! Organic Spirits

4065 West 11th Avenue, #47 ◆ (541) 255-7643
www.organicello.com
Saturday 2pm–7pm, Sunday 12 noon–5pm;
other times by appointment only
Driving time from Portland: about 2 hours

Crescendo! Organic Spirits was founded in 2013 by two engineers and veteran entrepreneurs who wanted to make liqueurs made with all-natural ingredients. The LimonCello is a limoncello, or lemon liqueur, originating from Southern Italy. Although it's been around for hundreds of years, it's a spirit that's underappreciated by most Americans, mostly because of an all-too-common encounter with overpriced, overly sweet versions. Crescendo!'s 'cellos—the LimonCello along with the LimeCello, a lime liqueur, and the AranCello, an orange liqueur—aren't cloyingly sweet. If you end up loving the products as much as the distillers do, you can invest in the company on Hatch Oregon, a resource for finding Community Public Offering investment opportunities. If you'd rather invest the traditional way, the tasting room serves cocktails made with its three products. Visit Crescendo! Organic Spirits and order one—or a few.

Tasting Menu: AranCello, LimeCello, LimonCello

High-Proof pick: The LimonCello is a classic formula that gives cocktails a citrusy brightness.

Elixir Craft Spirits
1050 Bethel Drive, #F3 and F4 • (541) 345-2257
www.elixir-us.com
Call ahead to schedule a tasting room visit
Driving time from Portland: about 2 hours

Elixir makes two truly unique craft spirits for the state of Oregon: Calisaya Liqueur and Iris Liqueur. The Calisaya is made from cinchona calisaya, a Peruvian shrub similar to quinine and once used to combat malaria. It was first brought to Rome by missionaries in 1632 and eventually became a favored liqueur throughout Italy and later in pre-Prohibition

America. The Iris Liqueur is made from—you guessed it—iris root. According to Elixir, Florentines cultivated iris plants to enhance wine and make floral liqueurs. The precious iris, also known as fleur-de-lis (French for "flower of the lily"), serves as the official emblem of Florence, even to this day, and was once a symbol of French royalty. Tip: If you're planning to try these two unique spirits while in Eugene, call ahead to schedule a visit.

> *Tasting Menu:* Calisaya Liqueur, Fernet dei Fratelli Loreto, Iris Liqueur

> *High-Proof pick:* Go for the Calisaya Liqueur, especially if you're a fan of modern-day medicinal liqueurs. It may be just the cure you're looking for.

HAPPY VALLEY

Eastside Distilling
Clackamas Town Center Tasting Room
12000 SE 82nd Avenue ♦ (503) 908-0637
Monday–Saturday, 10am–9pm; Sunday, 11am–7pm
Driving time from Portland: about 30 minutes

Heading to the Clackamas Town Center for some Cinnabon and Hot Topic? Don't pass up the Eastside Distilling tasting room. Tip: It's on the first level, so parking near Nordstrom and Sears is your best bet. The tasting room can also be used in negotiation tactics for those reluctant to go to a mall: "If you come with me, we'll go for a taster of spirits!" Who can resist?

> *Tasting Menu:* holiday liqueurs (Egg Nog 'Advocaat' Liqueur, Holiday Spiced Liqueur, Peppermint Bark Liqueur), rum (Below Deck Coffee Rum, Below Deck

Ginger Rum, Below Deck Silver Rum, Below Deck
Spiced Rum), vodka (Portland Potato Vodka), whiskey
(Barrel Hitch American Whiskey, Barrel Hitch Oregon
Oak American Whiskey, Burnside Bourbon, Cherry
Bomb Whiskey, Marionberry Whiskey, Oregon Oaked
Bourbon)

High-Proof pick: When in Clackamas, the answer is
whiskey. The Barrel Hitch American Whiskey will get
you through your day trip with its clean grain taste.

HILLSBORO

Big Bottom Distilling
21420 NW Nicholas Court, #9 • (503) 608-7816
www.bigbottomdistilling.com
Saturday, 12 noon–4pm; other times by appointment
Driving time from Portland: about 30 minutes

Ted Pappas created Big Bottom Whiskey in 2010 with intentions to be the premier independent bottler of whiskeys located in Hillsboro, Oregon. Since then, Big Bottom has added
fine gin, brandy, and whiskey. In 2017, Eastside Distilling pur-
chased a majority stake in Hillsboro's Big Bottom Distilling.
Tip: On the way over, you'll find yourself driving through a
large industrial park area. Don't worry; you're not lost. Just
keep driving to the end of the parking lot area, toward the
back of the industrial park.

Tasting Menu: brandy (apple, pear), gin (Barrel Aged
Gin, Oregon Gin, Navy Strength Gin), vodka (Starka
vodka), whiskey (Barlow Whiskey and Barlow Cask
Finish Whiskey, Delta Rye Whiskey, Warehouse Series
Bourbon Whiskey)

High-Proof pick: Try the Oregon Gin for a creamy oak flavor that bears little resemblance to classic gin formulas.

Cornelius Pass Roadhouse & Imbrie Hall Distillery

4045 NW Cornelius Pass Road ♦ (503) 640-6174
www.mcmenamins.com/CPR
Sunday–Monday, 11am–11pm; Tuesday–Thursday, 11am–12 midnight;
Friday–Saturday, 11am–1am
Driving time from Portland: about 30 minutes

The original buildings and barns—before they were converted to a pub and distillery—date all the way back to the 1850s. The historical site even houses a still that's one hundred and twenty years old, though McMenamins didn't start distilling here until 2011. Walk past Imbrie Hall and follow the path to the distillery area for a tour led by the head distiller. You'll be able to step inside the old barn that's been repurposed into a modern-day distillery. Savor the liquor and the history.

Tasting Menu: brandy (Morning Dew Brandy), liqueurs (Phil Hazelnut Liqueur), gin (Gables Gin), rum (Frank High Proof Rum), whiskey (Billy Whiskey, Devil's Bit Whiskey, White Owl Whiskey)

High-Proof pick: For seasonal sipping in the fall, try the Phil Hazelnut Liqueur. Fun fact: Ninety-nine percent of all hazelnuts grown in the U.S. are grown in the Willamette Valley in Oregon.

HOOD RIVER

Camp 1805
501 Portway Avenue, Suite #102 ◆ (541) 386-1805
www.camp1805.com
Monday–Thursday, 3pm–10pm; Friday, 3pm–11pm;
Saturday, 1pm-11pm; Sunday, 1pm–9pm
Driving time from Portland: under 1½ hours

Camp 1805 resembles what distilleries might eventually become: a full-on distillery pub. Camp 1805 has a complete bar menu, with cocktails and beer, as well as food and ample seating. It's also Hood River's first (new) rum and whiskey distillery since Prohibition.

> *Tasting Menu:* Backbone Rum, Endurance White Whiskey, Mt. Hood Vodka
>
> *High-Proof pick:* Try the Backbone Rum for an Oregon-made rum experience. It's very drinkable, and even if you prefer spirits with a kick, you'll love this rum.

Hood River Distillers
304 Oak Street, #3 ◆ (541) 386-1588, ext. 234
www.hrdspirits.com
Daily, 12 noon–6pm
Driving time from Portland: under 1½ hours

In the eighty-plus years since Hood River Distillers was established (in 1934), it has achieved a lot, including creating an extensive portfolio and procuring international distribution—all while continuing to bottle in Oregon. It's no surprise, then, that Hood River Distillers is the Northwest's largest and oldest importer, producer, and bottler of distilled spirits, doing everything at its current facility since 1969. The development of the company's portfolio includes spirits like Lucid Absinthe Supérieure (a genuine absinthe made with real grand wormwood), ULLR Nordic Libation (a peppermint-flavored liquor), Yazi Ginger Flavored Vodka, and Clear Creek Distillery McCarthy's Oregon Single Malt Whiskey. The tasting room at Hood River is a warm and inviting place to try local and international spirits imported from all over the world.

> *Tasting* Menu: absinthe, (Jade 1901 Absinthe Supérieur, Lucid Absinthe Supérieure), gin (Captive Spirits Big Gin), vodka (44° North Vodka, HRD Vodka, Yazi Ginger), whiskey (McCarthy's Oregon Single Malt Whiskey, Pendleton 1910 Rye Whisky, Pendleton Midnight Whisky, Pendleton Directors' Reserve, Pendleton Whisky, Sinfire Cinnamon Whisky, Trail's End Bourbon), Monarch Brands, ULLR Nordic Libation)

> *High-Proof pick:* For a spirit finished by Hood River Distillers, ask for the Kentucky Straight Bourbon Whiskey, a whiskey aged eight years and finished in Oregon oak barrels.

MᶜMINNVILLE

Ransom Spirits
525 NE Third Street (tasting room only) • (503) 876-5022
www.ransomspirits.com
Thursday, 11am–5pm; Friday–Saturday, 11am-7pm; Sunday, 11am–5pm
Driving time from Portland: about 1 hour

From Ransom Spirits' forty-acre production facility in nearby Sheridan, Oregon (the McMinnville location is a tasting room only), this wine and spirits company creates all of its distillates by taste and smell rather than by the use of high-tech equipment and gauges. What you see is what you get, and Ransom shows it all—in a good way. On the front of most of Ransom's bottles, you can see all of the ingredients used to produce that particular spirit. Ransom Spirits are produced with tradition and transparency in mind, but the execution—its overall taste, branding, and marketing—feels fresh and modern.

Tasting Menu: gin (Ransom Dry Gin, Ransom Old Tom Gin), grappa (Gewürztraminer Grappa), vodka (The Vodka), whiskey (Emerald 1865 Straight American Whisky, Henry DuYore's Rye Whiskey, Rye, Barley, Wheat Whiskey, WhipperSnapper Oregon Spirit Whiskey)

High-Proof pick: The pleasant aroma and smoothness of the Gewürztraminer Grappa will change your mind about grappa—or make up your mind if you previously knew nothing about this grape-based brandy. Try the Ransom Old Tom Gin for an Old World taste made with Oregon-grown aromatics and botanicals.

NEWPORT

Rogue House of Spirits
2122 SE Marine Science Drive ◆ (541) 867-3660
www.rogue.com
Hours vary by season
Driving time from Portland: under 3 hours

Visit one of the first distillery pubs in America with sweeping views of the Yaquina Bay Marina, Bay Bridge, and Pacific Ocean. From Rogue's Newport distillery pub, you'll find a full selection of its award-winning spirits, in addition to its ales, lagers, porters, and stouts.

Tasting Menu: gin (Pink Spruce Gin, Spruce Gin), rum (Dark Rum, Hazelnut Spice Rum, White Rum), whiskey (Chipotle Whiskey, Dead Guy Whiskey, Oregon Single Malt Whiskey, Rogue Farms Oregon Rye Whiskey), vodka (Oregon Single Malt Vodka, Voodoo Bacon Maple Vodka)

High-Proof pick: For a bright-tasting pick-me-up, order a Pink Gin & Juice, a cocktail made with Pink Spruce Gin, grapefruit juice, and orange juice. Also, don't forget to try a beer while you're there. The Dead Guy Ale is a classic choice.

TIGARD

Indio Spirits Distillery and Tasting Room
7272 SW Durham Road, #100 ♦ (503) 620-0313
www.indiospirits.com
Thursday, 3pm–8pm, Friday–Saturday, 2pm–7pm,
Sunday 12 noon–4pm
Driving time from Portland: about 30 minutes

Portland Tasting Room and Bottle Shop
1111 SW Alder St, Portland, OR, 97205
Wednesday-Saturday, 12 noon–8pm, Sunday, 12 noon–4pm

Indio Spirits produces a wide selection of unique vodka, rum, and liqueurs not produced by anyone else in the state. From its quiet and tidy tasting room in Tigard, try selections like Lemongrass Lime Vodka, Hopka Hop Liqueur, Barrel Room Curaçao, Starka Barrel Aged Vodka, and Red Island Finger Lime Rum. In 2016 Indio opened a tasting room in downtown Portland, bringing their spirits to Bridgetown while keeping the spirits production in Tigard.

Tasting Menu: Barrel Room Curaçao, gin (Cricket Club Gin), liqueurs (Hopka Hop Liqueur), rum (Barrel Room Rum, Red Island Black Spiced Rum, Red Island Finger Lime Rum), vodka (Blood Orange, Lemongrass Lime, Marionberry, Starka Barrel Aged, Premium Silver Vodka), whiskey (James Oliver American, James Oliver Rye, Snake River Stampede, Snake River Stampede Small Batch)

High-Proof pick: The Hopka Hop Liqueur is on the sweeter side, but it's something you won't see at other distilleries.

TROUTDALE

McMenamins Edgefield Distillery
2126 SW Halsey Street ◆ (503) 492-5442
www.mcmenamins.com/878-edgefield-distillery-home
Daily tours at 2pm
Driving time from Portland: about 30 minutes

Since February 1998, the McMenamins Edgefield Distillery in Troutdale has been not only the birthplace of many spirits but also the birthplace of many distillers' careers. Christian Krogstad of House Spirits and Lee Medoff of Bull Run Distilling Company both got their start here. Catch a tour of the dry-shed, which was once used to store vegetables and produce and now is the site where the bulk of the spirits made by the McMenamins chain is produced, with the exception of batches made at the Cornelius Pass Roadhouse & Imbrie Hall Distillery. Calling it a tour might even be an overstatement since the space is small; in fact, there's little to no walking on this tour. The lack of square footage here is impressive, though, when you consider that the company makes a helluva lot of booze at this space. On the other side of what looks like a barn wall, you can order full-size cocktails made with Edgefield spirits.

Tasting Menu: brandy (Alambic "13" Brandy, Edgefield Brandy, Longshot Brandy, Pear Brandy), gin (Joe Penney's Gin), liqueur (coffee, Herbal Liqueur No. 7), rum (Three Rocks Rum, Three Rocks Spiced Rum) whiskey (Aval Pota Whiskey, Hogshead Whiskey, Monkey Puzzle Whiskey)

High-Proof pick: Try the Billy Whiskey, a wheat whiskey made in McMenamins' century-old alembic still and aged two years in charred oak barrels.

USE THE HASHTAG
#HIGHPROOFROADTRIP
TO CHRONICLE YOUR
DRINKING ADVENTURES
OUTSIDE OF THE CITY ON
SOCIAL MEDIA.

2.

THE
AFTER PARTY

THE
AFTER PARTY

COCKTAIL BARS
THE HOME BAR
HANGOVER CURES

Y ou've sampled Portland's best craft spirits.
Now, create cocktails to experience spirits
in a new way. Get your home bar started
or explore the city's hottest cocktail bars.

HIGH-PROOF PICKS THE BEST COCKTAIL BARS IN PORTLAND

Portland has long been known for its beer. Now the buzz around the city's cuisine is set to eclipse beer; Bon Appétit magazine loves us, and our chefs consistently win national awards. So what's the next big thing for Portland?

Spurred forward by the availability and quality of local craft spirits and cocktail ingredients, the Bridgetown cocktail scene is earning accolades and growing a reputation outside of the city too. Just as Portland chefs have earned global repute, our stellar bartenders are pushing the boundaries in cocktail mixing with new combinations and refined techniques that are getting a lot of people's attention. Try the works of the masters at these Portland cocktail bars.

Angel Face

14 NE 28th Avenue ◆ (503) 239-3804
www.angelfaceportland.com
Sunday–Thursday, 5pm–12 midnight; Friday–Saturday, 5pm–1am

Depending on your level of cocktail enthusiasm, Angel Face will either delight you or infuriate you. There's no elaborate cocktail menu here; in fact, there's no cocktail menu at all. Instead, you bring the menu. You sit down, tell them what kind of spirit you like or what kind of taste you're looking for (sour, sweet, floral, etc.), and the bartenders make you a cocktail to satisfy your cravings. I love how Angel Face gives you control by letting you choose the elements, and then takes that control away by crafting something mysterious and complex.

Ava Gene's

3377 SE Division Street ◆ (971) 229-0571 ◆ www.avagenes.com
Monday–Thursday, 5pm–10pm; Friday–Saturday, 5pm–11pm;
Sunday, 4:30pm–10pm

Cocktail-minded folks like us know the importance of a cocktail menu when contemplating dinner reservations. It usually goes something like this: first, you hear that a place is said to have a killer menu. Next, you read reviews in national magazines. From there, you decide to give the restaurant a try, but not before first perusing the cocktail menu to ensure there are at least three concoctions that fit the bill. Ava Gene's is that kind of place where it's hard to nab a table, but once you do, you'll be perfectly satisfied by both the food and the cocktails. The fare is Roman-inspired with an emphasis on local and a full drinking experience to complement the top-notch food.

Besaw's

1545 NW 21st Avenue ◆ (503) 228-2619 ◆ www.besaws.com
Monday–Friday, 7am–3pm and 5pm–10 pm;
Saturday–Sunday, 8am–3pm and 5pm–10 pm

The history of Besaw's dates back to 1903 when George Besaw and Medric Liberty dreamed of starting their own beer parlor and gambling hall. Henry Weinhard, the legendary brewer, helped foot the bill for the opening of this neighborhood watering hole. After the repeal of Prohibition, Besaw's was the first bar in the state of Oregon to be granted a liquor license. A Portland institution for its longevity, Besaw's is also known for its menu that includes pan-seared meatloaf and breakfast comforts like pancakes and Eggs Benedict. It's also known for its long lines and trendy NW 23rd Avenue location. Recently, the popular brunch spot's story took a bittersweet turn. In 2016, Besaw's landlord decided not to renew its lease. After one hundred and twelve years of business, Besaw's shut its doors and moved to a new location on NW 21st Avenue. Luckily, it still offers the same classics but in a new, expanded space.

The Bible Club

6716 SE 16th Avenue, (971) 279-2198 ◆ www.bibleclubpdx.com
Sunday, 4–11pm, Wednesday–Thursday, 5pm–12am,
Friday–Saturday, 5pm–1am

While looking for The Bible Club, keep your eye out for the glowing light on the second floor of the yellow house, as you won't see an obvious sign. As you open the front door, you will be greeted by a pre-Prohibition-era museum of sconces, doillies, and glassware. Even the soundtrack is from the 1880s to 1920s. The speakeasy offers a menu of excellently crafted fruit-forward, spirit driven, and herbaceous cocktails. The tongue-in-cheek name might keep the general public at bay, which just means more seats at the bar for us.

Bit House Saloon

727 SE Grand Avenue ✦ (503) 954-3913
www.bithousesaloon.com ✦ Daily, 3pm–2:30am

Ever-changing and idiosyncratic ingredients like snap pea shrubs, corn milk, and liquid nitrogen are served in cocktails here alongside basic drinks like Miller High Life. The Bit House signature cocktails are organized in four categories: adventurous, refreshing, low proof, and carbonated. Some of the concoctions are slightly peculiar on paper but structured in execution. There are also upgraded basics like the Bit House Manhattan made with Weller Special Reserve Single Barrel Whiskey, a house vermouth blend, and bitters. There's also an entire menu of boilermakers. Bit House's building itself is distinctive; the bar opened in the summer of 2015, but the structure dates back to 1896.

The Box Social

3971 N Williams Avenue (503) 288-1111 ✦ www.bxsocial.com
Daily, 4pm–2am

The Box Social is a cozy North Portland bar known for its craft cocktails with a good mix of Portland spirits here, in addition to imports. The vibe most nights is very dark and very chill. So dark in fact, people often get in "the mood" to hang out in the bathrooms together. Signs near the sinks ask patrons to refrain from using the edges of the pedestal sinks as support for their sexual endeavors.

Clyde Common

1014 SW Stark Street ✦ (503) 228-3333 ✦ www.clydecommon.com
Monday–Thursday, 11:30am–11:45pm; Friday, 11:30am–
12:45am; Saturday, 10am–12:45am; Sunday, 10am–11:45pm

This European-style tavern and restaurant, adjacent to the Ace

Hotel, is a key player in Portland's cocktail scene, thanks to high standards of service and a damn fine menu. All this is due to Jeffrey Morgenthaler, a bar manager and drink writer, who was hired in 2009. After Jeffrey came on board, he hired new bar staff, retrained existing bartenders, and refreshed the menu, solidifying the Clyde Common standards we see today. Barrel-aged, bottled, and small-batch creations round out Jeffrey's drinks menu, which is chock-full of spirits any cocktail lover should know, such as Amontillado sherry, Aperol, Becherovka, Campari, and Cynar, among others. Add Clyde Common to your bucket list—or don't consider yourself a proper cocktail enthusiast.

Driftwood Room

729 SW 15th Avenue, inside Hotel DeLuxe
www.hoteldeluxeportland.com/eat-drink/driftwood-room
Monday–Thursday, 2pm–11:30pm; Friday, 2pm–12:30am;
Saturday, 10am–12:30am; Sunday, 10am–11:30pm

Since the 1950s, the Driftwood Room, located inside Hotel DeLuxe, has been a bastion of old-school cocktails and other classic libations made with Portland (and Oregon) ingredients. The bar's interior exudes a mid-century vibe—and the same goes for the cocktails. Despite the Mad Men charm, the bartenders at Driftwood keep it modern and cutting-edge. The menu is routinely updated with ingredients made or grown by local purveyors like Bee Local Honey, Jacobsen Salt Co., Smith Teamaker, and so on. Expect new takes on old favorites like the Sazerac made with a simple syrup that uses Smith Teamaker Hibiscus Tea, and the Old Tom made with Ransom Spirits Old Tom Gin, Agwa de Bolivia Liqueur, House Spirits Distillery Krogstad Aquavit, lime juice, and barrel-aged bitters.

Expatriate

5424 NE 30th Avenue • www.expatriatepdx.com
Daily, 5pm–12 midnight

Although I'm as happy as a razor clam here in Portland, the word "expatriate" excites me. The thought of packing up for Southeast Asia, never to return to the States, is worthy of more than a few daydreams. It's not about running away, though; it's about immersing yourself in another country until it becomes your new home. That's what Expatriate feels like for me. As Portland bars go, it's foreign enough to excite me, but it's also approachable enough that I could stay and become a regular. Kyle Linden Webster mans the ship here, mixing up skillfully crafted cocktails, as well as tunes from a vinyl record collection on rotation. Snacks and brunch at the bar come from Naomi Pomeroy, who runs Beast, a restaurant across the street.

The Fireside NW

801 NW 23rd Avenue • (503) 477-9505 • www.pdxfireside.com
Monday–Thursday, 11:30am–10pm;
Friday–Saturday, 11:30am–12 midnight; Sunday, 10am–3pm;
Happy Hour, Monday–Friday only, 3pm–5:30pm

Fireside is co-owned by Sue Erickson, the resident bartender since 2005 and a contributor to Portland's drinking scene. The quintessential Northwest fare shouldn't be missed either. Watch a real fire crackle from two indoor fireplaces in the dining room and bar while you sip your drinks and eat. Tip: Roll in for the generous happy hour for $6 cocktails and bar snacks under $10.

The Green Room at Multnomah Whiskey Library

1122 SW Alder Street (street level) • (503) 954-1381
www.mwlpdx.com
Monday–Thursday, 4pm–12 midnight; Friday–Saturday, 4pm–1am

Non-members waiting to get into Multnomah Whiskey Library can get around the long waits by going to The Green Room instead. The Green Room boasts the same level of quality and selection you expect from the Library, as well as a reassuring level of hype. The difference is you can enjoy a few cocktails here and get out in less than an hour. The drinks made in The Green Room are weaker in strength (on the low proof side) than what you'd generally get at the Library—which isn't always a bad thing, you animal. At The Green Room, you can drink cocktails made with sherries, aperitifs, bitters, and liqueurs to keep you satiated but not too drunk, before you head up the stairs to the Library.

Hale Pele

2733 NE Broadway Street ◆ (503) 662-8454 ◆ www.halepele.com
Sunday–Thursday 4pm–12 midnight; Friday–Saturday, 4pm–1am

The somewhat underground Tiki following in the U.S. recognizes Hale Pele as one of the best Tiki bars in the country. Outside of the guava, coconut, and all encompassing culture, though, it's also an overall favorite in Portland. There's an extensive menu of rum from all over the world here, and a playful menu that rates the strength of its drinks "1 (lightly delightful) to 4 (KA-BOOM)." (As a reference, the Piña Colada is ranked a "2," or "pleasantly punch.") Hale Pele owner Blair Reynolds is also the creator of premium B.G. Reynolds Syrups. Tiki culture, though, is so much more than just the drinks; it's also about the kitsch, clothing, barware, and food. For a solid snack, try the Pu-Pus. The Hawaiian bread, made by local family business Lilikoi Bakery, and served with a luscious guava jam made with B.G. Reynolds Vanilla and Ginger Syrups. It's often referred to as "crack bread" because it's just that addicting.

Hamlet

232 NW 12th Avenue ◆ (503) 241-4009 ◆ www.hamletpdx.com
Monday–Thursday, 4pm–11pm; Friday–Saturday, 4pm–1am

A ham bar. Hamlet is a ham bar. What does this mean? It means prosciutto and other fine slices of pig are served next to and incorporated alongside cocktails. Come here to order some fine meats, such as the vertically sliced speck, aged for twelve months, or to drink intriguing cocktails, such as the glorious Thumper's Revenge, a drink made with house-made horseradish vodka, freshly pressed lime juice, freshly extracted carrot juice, and house-blended clover honey syrup. You really can't go wrong with any of the drink offerings here, but if you want to do it right, order the cocktail that has ham as an ingredient: the Melon vs. Meat. Hamlet is the creation of bartender Ryan Magarian and Cathy Whims of Oven and Shaker, located just around the corner.

Kachka

720 SE Grand Avenue ◆ (503) 235-0059 ◆ www.kachkapdx.com
Daily, 4pm–10pm; Happy Hour, 4pm–6pm & 10pm–12 midnight

Zakuski. Pelmeni. And vodka. It's the holy trifecta and the way of life at Kachka, Portland's upscale Russian joint that serves traditional dumplings, cold and hot zakuski, an array of main dishes, and a ton of pickled goodness. Kachka teamed up with New Deal Distillery to take its horseradish-infused vodka to the next level, and now Kachka Horseradish Vodka is bottled and distilled at New Deal and available for purchase at liquor stores across the city.

Lantern Lounge and Eatery

726 SE Grand Avenue ◆ (503) 232-1532 ◆ www.lanternpdx.com
Sunday, 5pm–12am, Tuesday–Thursday, 5pm–12 midnight;
Friday–Saturday, 5pm– 12am; Sunday, 5pm–12 midnight

Inside Lantern, neon red letters affixed to the wall spell out its name and cast a red glow along with red paper lanterns that hang from the ceiling. Hints of the lounge's drink, food and decor inspired by Vietnam are apparent but pleasantly subdued, like condensed milk in a cocktail that also incorporates vodka, velvet falernum, apple, lime, and toasted marshmallow. Whether it's authentically Vietnamese doesn't even need to be up for debate: the vibe here will take you out of Portland and into a dark cocktail lounge in another place.

Rue

1005 SE Ankeny Street ◆ (503) 231-3748 ◆ www.ruepdx.com
Tuesday–Thursday, 5pm–11pm; Friday–Saturday, 4pm–11pm

In the mood for bitter and herbaceous, cool and refreshing, or spirit forward? Rue's brilliantly organized menu makes deciding what to order that much easier. Bar manager Jon Lewis, ensures the cocktails are visually appealing too, often layering beautifully hued spirits and ice in a playful way.

Pépé le Moko

407 SW 10th Avenue ◆ (503) 546-8537
www.pepelemokopdx.com
Daily, 4pm–2am

Only a handful of bars in Portland can claim speakeasy status, and Pépé le Moko is one of them. Hidden in the dark underbelly of Clyde Common, this bar offers classic-as-can-be cocktails like the Long Island Ice Tea, Grasshopper, or Amaretto Sour, all made just for you by the inimitable Jeffrey Morgenthaler, the man who brought barrel-aged Manhattans to Portland and overhauled Clyde Common's well-respected menu. Tip: The entrance to Pépé le Moko isn't through Clyde Common but on 10th Avenue.

The Rookery Bar at Raven & Rose ━━━━━━━
1331 SW Broadway ◆ (503) 222-7673
www.ravenandrosepdx.com
Tuesday–Wednesday, 4pm–10pm;
Thursday–Friday, 4pm–12 midnight; Saturday, 5pm–12 midnight

Raven & Rose is located in the Ladd Carriage House, one of the last remaining buildings from the William Ladd Estate. (William Ladd owned local flour mills, was a purveyor of liquor, and formed the Portland Water Commission.) The Carriage House was built in 1883 and is one of the last examples of English Stick architecture in the country. On the second floor of the restaurant is the Rookery Bar. Climb the stairs to this fancy "tree house" filled with interesting furniture and décor like leather upholstery, beautiful slabs of wood and marble, and exposed beams. While there, sip cocktails made with single-barrel whiskey selected by the staff and bottled exclusively for the Rookery Bar's cocktail menu, which includes drinks like the Debutante, made with Oregon-produced Ransom Spirits Old Tom Gin, Germain-Robin Heirloom Apple Brandy, grenadine, lemon, honey, and egg white.

Rum Club ━━━━━━━━━━━━━━━━━━
720 SE Sandy Boulevard ◆ (503) 265-8807
www.rumclubpdx.com ◆ Daily, 4pm–2am

When you think of daiquiris, you probably think of a pink frozen cocktail in a plastic Hurricane glass. At Rum Club, daiquiris are classier than this. Here, the classic cocktail is a far cry from the one your Aunt drank on her last Carnival Cruise trip—it's made just the way it was made for Ernest Hemingway. The

Rum Club Daiquiri is made with aged rum, fresh lime juice, rich simple syrup, maraschino liqueur, Angostura Bitters, and Herbsaint. It's a little bit tropical, a little bit Portland. Within the cocktail scene, Rum Club is a venerable institution for not only its daiquiri but also for its highly-regarded techniques in mixing and creating cocktails.

The Solo Club

2110 NW Raleigh Street ◆ (971) 254-9806
www.thesoloclub.com
Sunday, 8am–10pm; Tuesday–Thursday, 3pm–12 midnight;
Friday, 3pm–1am; Saturday, 8am to 1am

The star libations at The Solo Club are of the bitter variety. Amari and vermouth are the backbone of cocktails throughout the menu served in this vibrant, café by day, and bar by evening establishment. A Southeast-Asian inspired menu plays well with delightfully bitter and excellently produced cocktails. The drinks aren't overly complex but the ingredients can be. Similar to life in a South Asian beach town, you can step back from the complexity offered here if you choose. Straightforward coolers like a Spritz are made to order from Cava and your choice of amaro.

Tannery Bar

5425 E Burnside Street ◆ (503) 236-3610
www.tannerybarpdx.com
Monday–Saturday, 4pm–1am; Saturday–Sunday 9am–2pm

This hidden North Tabor neighborhood bar makes up for its lack of dive bar staples like Kitty Glitter slots, Keno, and Oregon Lottery Scratch-Its with extravagant cocktails from the bar made with ingredients like Zwack Unicum Herbal Liqueur and Old Weller 107. You'd expect to see a place serving cocktails like these on a street lined with trendy boutiques.

Instead, it's located across the street from a Quality Food Center and is surrounded by residential homes. Regardless of its setting, Tannery works it and should be a destination on your list as it is for many Portland cocktail buffs.

Teardrop Lounge
1015 NW Everett Street ◆ (503) 445-8109
www.teardroplounge.com
Daily, 4pm–closing; Happy Hour, Monday–Friday only, 4pm–7pm

Teardrop Lounge is an old-school staple in the Portland drinking scene. Those who prefer lowball and coupe glasses to steins and pint glasses have been pulling up a chair around the liquid drop-shaped bar for years. Daniel Shoemaker is a name to know as you start reaching "Full-Blown Pundit" cocktail enthusiast level.

Not only has he helped countless bars in the city launch successful cocktail programs, but his own menu is also updated constantly with new medleys made up of house-made bitters and other concoctions.

Whey Bar at Ox Restaurant
2225 NE Martin Luther King Jr. Boulevard ◆ (503) 284-3366
www.oxpdx.com
Daily, 4pm–closing

Ox Restaurant is a big deal in Portland. It's one of a growing number of "bucket list" restaurants that food lovers have at the top of their must-try lists. It's likely someone has demanded, "You haven't been there yet?" if you have, in fact, not been. Not getting into Ox isn't the worst-case scenario, though. To this day, Whey Bar is one of my favorite discoveries. It was here that I had my first cocktail with whey as an ingredient: the Whey of the Gun. This singular drink is made with Jamaican rum, bourbon, whey, and lime. It's also the home to the Ox Blood, a beautifully hued drink made with bourbon, beet syrup, lemon, and tarragon. On top of extraordinary cocktail ingredients, there's an oyster bar too. Whey Bar is a spot to decompress while you wait for dinner at Ox, but it's definitely worth visiting all on its own.

SETTING UP YOUR HOME BAR

Is this you?

You can spot Cash & Carry olives from across the bar; in fact, you prefer the Castelvetrano. You know that the better Maraschino cherries should be made with Luxardo liqueur. You've gripped more than a few coupe glasses in your day. When you see Chartreuse on the menu, you know there's a chance creatively mixed drinks are on the horizon.

If so, or if you just want to get a handle on your home bar, then you'll appreciate this chapter. Here, you'll find a guide to becoming a Portland cocktail epicurean. You'll learn about where to shop for fancy barware, syrups, and mixers for your home bartending needs, or where to get local ingredients to add complexity to your homemade cocktails. You'll also find out about other palate-pleasing Portland-made hooch. Finally, you'll learn about events like TOAST and Feast Portland that bring local distillers together to showcase and celebrate their high-proof wares.

BAR TOOLS: THE BASICS

While Bull in China and other stores make beautiful barware, your best bet may be to head to

LEVELS OF COCKTAIL ENTHUSIASM

I'll drink it as long as I can't taste the whiskey.
    —The Maturing Adherent

Soda water and lime instead of tonic, please.
        —The Budding Snob

The ingredients and the hand that mixed this make this drink worth $14.
        —The Full-Blown Pundit

a restaurant supply store, especially when you're just starting out. Restaurant supply stores are fantastic places to find metal tumblers or spoons. Also, if you find yourself needing pint glasses, try one of Portland's many fine thrift stores.

Here are some of the supplies that you'll want to stock your home bar with to make cocktails at home:

bar spoon
Generally speaking, if you're making a cocktail using all spirits (no mixers) or clear spirits, you'll want to stir and not shake to get a cocktail with the best look and mouthfeel. Use a bar spoon to stir. Bar spoons are longer than regular spoons and have a threaded stem. You can also use a bar spoon to make a swizzle cocktail with crushed ice.

jigger
Think of the jigger as a shot glass for measuring. Jiggers are metal, hourglass-shaped measuring devices with dual measuring "cups," usually 1 ounce and ½ ounce, or 1 and ½ ounces and ¾ ounce.

muddler
The muddler is a stick used for mashing and crushing ingredients in a cocktail. Look for muddlers made with unvarnished wood or metal.

shaker
There are two kinds of shakers: the cobbler shaker and the Boston shaker. The cobbler shaker is the shaker that every cocktail enthusiast gets for Christmas because it looks fancy. They're commonly made up of a metal tumbler, a metal lid with a built in strainer, and a cap. Boston shakers are more common among professional bartenders. It's made up of a metal tumbler

and a pint glass. If you're serious about making cocktails, leave the cobbler shaker on the bar for looks and
upgrade to the Boston shaker.

strainer

There are two basic types of strainers: Hawthorne
and Julep. The Hawthorne has a flexible spring that
catches ice and is most common. The Julep strainer
is less common and is a perforated bowl-shaped cup
with a handle. For the average home bartender, the
Hawthorne will work just fine.

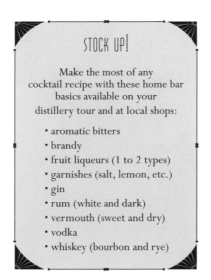

STOCK UP!

Make the most of any
cocktail recipe with these home bar
basics available on your
distillery tour and at local shops:

- aromatic bitters
- brandy
- fruit liqueurs (1 to 2 types)
- garnishes (salt, lemon, etc.)
- gin
- rum (white and dark)
- vermouth (sweet and dry)
- vodka
- whiskey (bourbon and rye)

PREPARING FOR YOUR SHOPPING TRIP

Oregon Liquor Search
www.oregonliquorsearch.com

If you're a distillery tourist and not an actual tourist, meaning you live in Oregon, I encourage you to buy bottles for your home bar from distilleries if you are able to transport them home safely. If you don't think you can transport your new purchases home from the distillery, you still have options. Liquor stores in Oregon are controlled by The Oregon Liquor Control Commission (OLCC), which also means that the OLCC is often a distiller's biggest customer. Head to www.oregonliquorsearch.com if you know which spirit you're looking for and the website will tell you which Oregon liquor store you can find it.

The Crafted Life
www.crafted-life.com

The Crafted Life is a joint venture between a professional marketing agency and an event management and publishing consultancy to promote the sales of local Oregon spirits online. What does this mean for you? It means if you're a tourist (an actual tourist, not being derogatory here) you can take note of the spirits you liked and then have them shipped home to you after you've arrived. You'll still be supporting the distillery and the craft spirits movement, and you won't have to worry about a broken bottle and a booze soaked suitcase.

SHOP

One thing I love about living in Portland is that you can buy nearly everything you need for your home bar right here in the city. Then, you can meet the maker at an event or farmer's market, follow the maker on Instagram or Twitter, and really know where the products you love come from (and creep on cat photos too).

For any cocktail, the rule is the elements like the salts, bitters, syrups, and garnishes matter just as much as the spirits and methods used to make the drink. Here are some of the best local businesses making those crucial additions to your cocktail recipes.

Bull in China

2109 NW Irving Street ◆ (971) 888-4085
www.bullinchinapdx.com
Wednesday–Saturday, 12 noon–6pm
Visit by appointment only or shop online

This finely crafted barware company started out as a hobby for collecting vintage barware. This passion later turned into product development, starting first with mixing glass and then extending to a line of ice mallets, stirred drink sets, bitters bottles, and other items. The company's mixing glasses are spot-on and can be a beautiful addition to your home bar. Like the newbie pizza employee practicing with a wet rag before throwing dough into the air, you better practice with old glassware first.

The Meadow

3731 N Mississippi Avenue ◆ (503) 974-8349
Daily, 10am–8pm
805 NW 23rd Avenue ◆ (503) 305-3388
Sunday–Thursday, 10am–8pm; Friday–Saturday, 10am–9pm
www.themeadow.com

With two locations in North Portland and Northwest Portland, and more than a hundred salts, seven hundred chocolates, and two-hundred and eighty bitters, it's more than likely you'll discover something new and arcane here for your next cocktail experiment. But wait—there's more! Reverse-engineered recipes from the 1800s, products from local producers, and the bitters that played a role in the American cocktail revival can all be found here too.

Pearl Specialty Market

900 NW Lovejoy Street, #140 ◆ (503) 477-8604
www.pearlspecialty.com
Monday–Saturday, 9am–10pm; Sunday, 12 noon–8pm

With one of the largest selection of bitters in the country (over seventy varieties and growing), including brands like Bittermens, Dram, Fee Brothers, and The Bitter End, and a wide variety of vermouth, mixers, and garnishes, Pearl Specialty Market has nearly everything for your cocktail needs. It also features high-end items like Toschi Amarina and Amarena Fabbri Wild Cherries in Syrup, and even the not so high-end but sometimes essential items like Jose Cuervo Margarita Salt.

Bee Local Honey

602 SE Salmon Street ◆ (503) 619-5609 ◆ www.beelocal.com
Monday–Friday, 9am–5pm
Buy online, at the tasting room, or at retailers

In 2011, Damian Magista discovered that honey from beehives around Portland had different flavor profiles based on the neighborhood: less or more sweet, fruity, and so on.
Bee Local is sold nationally but harvested locally.
Add a touch of local floral sweetness to your cocktails using Bee Local Honey instead of the more common agave syrups, which often have added high fructose corn syrup. While here, grab salts from Jacobsen Salt Co. too.

> High-Proof pick: Single Origin Willamette Valley Honey. Represent.

B.G. Reynolds

www.bgreynolds.com
Buy online through its exclusive network of distributors listed at
www.bgreynolds.com/ordering/

Tiki love is strong in Portland and across the region. The small but devoted community of Tiki fans in the Pacific Northwest has turned that love into Tiki Kon, an annual symposium of all things Polynesian. For the other fifty-one weekends out of the year, Tiki aficionados can turn to Blair Reynolds's bar Hale Pele or to his line of syrups, produced under the name B.G. Reynolds.

> High-Proof pick: The syrups are a perfect addition to your tropical-themed cocktails. Pick up the Passion Fruit, Orgeat (think: Mai Tai cocktails), or Lush Grenadine.

The Bitter Housewife ━━━━━━━━━━━━━━━━━━━━

www.thebitterhousewife.com
Buy online or at retailers

Genevieve Brazelton, a former San Francisco bar manager, created The Bitter Housewife Bitters to make cocktails more fun and approachable. Use these bitters generously, more so than other bitters. Where you might only use a few dashes of your standard highly concentrated bitters, you can use nearly three times the amount of Bitter Housewife bitters. This means the flavors are more forgiving for the home bartender who's just starting out. The Bitter Housewife acquired RAFT Botanical Cocktail + Soda Syrup in 2016, expanding its lineup of options for cocktail enthusiasts.

> High-Proof pick: Some of my favorite flavors include Grapefruit, Aromatic, and Cardamom Bitters. For a truly Portland collaboration though, go for the Barrel-Aged Aromatic Bitters, a rich, flavorful pairing of Bull Run Distilling Company Temperance Trader American Whiskey and Bitter Housewife Aromatic Bitters.

The Commissary ━━━━━━━━━━━━━━━━━━━━

www.commissarypdx.com
Buy at Pearl Specialty Market or online

The Commissary is a juicing and syrup-making business. Fresh, unpasteurized juice is pressed daily here and sold to both bars and home bar enthusiasts. Check out the extensive handmade syrup selection, which ranges from simple syrups and fruit-flavored syrups, to grenadine and oleo-saccharum syrups, the perfect base for many classic punches.

> High-Proof pick: Pick up some oleo-saccharum syrup for a classic punch. This sugared oil is delicious in more than punches too. (Bonus: With a bottle in your arsenal,

you won't have to zest any lemons on your own.)

Imbue

www.imbuecellars.com
Buy online or at retailers

The word "imbue" means to inspire or permeate with a feeling or quality. Imbue embodies this as Portland's premier vermouth maker, making two must-have craft vermouths. The Bittersweet Vermouth uses Oregon-grown pinot gris and Clear Creek Distillery-made pinot gris brandy aged in American oak casks. It has nine botanicals that impart flavors like elderflower, pear, and vanilla. The Petal & Thorn is similar to the Bittersweet Vermouth, except it includes ten botanicals like chamomile and orange peel, as well as Oregon-grown beets, which gives it its charming pink hue. Imbue's two aperitifs will infuse your craft gin and vodka with wonderfully complex flavors.

High-Proof pick: Try both. Sip the Bittersweet Vermouth neat to taste its pleasing sweetness and bitterness. Add the Petal & Thorn to ice and seltzer water for a simple yet flavorful drink that impresses.

Jacobsen Salt Co.

602 SE Salmon Street • (503) 473-3952 • www.jacobsenseasalt.com
Monday–Friday, 9am–5pm
Buy online, at the tasting room, or at retailers

When using high-end spirits and other ingredients for your cocktails, it would be a travesty to salt the rim of your cocktail glass with something as mundane as Morton Salt—not when there's a local harvester selling irresistible salts from Netarts Bay, an area five miles south of Tillamook, Oregon. Up your cocktail game with Jacobsen's infused salts like the Gold Label

Cacao Salt, Lemon Zest Flake Salt, Negroni Cocktail Salt, Oregon Pinot Noir Flake Salt, or Pinot Blanc Flake Salt. If you visit the tasting room, don't forget to drop by Bee Local Honey housed in the same building.

> High-Proof pick: With notes of juniper berry and orange, the Negroni Cocktail Salt will round out your home bar experience.

RAFT Botanical Cocktail + Soda Syrup •————————
www.raftsyrups.com
Buy online or at retailers

RAFT, now owned by The Bitter Housewife, offers three complex syrups: Smoked Tea Vanilla, Hibiscus Lavender, and Lemon Ginger. For a generous 250 ml bottle of botanically infused syrup goodness, you'll pay only $14.99. Tip: Try your hand at the Smoky Pineapple Delight, a cocktail made with RAFT Smoked Tea Vanilla syrup and New Deal Distillery Hot Monkey Vodka. The recipe is available online at www.raftsyrups.com/recipes.

> High-Proof pick: The Lemon Ginger syrup is versatile and uncomplicated enough to use in many cocktails.

FOR COCKTAIL RECIPES
USING LOCAL SPIRITS
VISIT
WWW.HIGHPROOFPDX.COM

Pok Pok Som

www.shop.pokpoksom.com
Buy online or at retailers

Pok Pok Som offers a selection of sweet and tart drinking vinegars made by Chef Andy Ricker, a James Beard Award winner, Thai food aficionado, founder of the renowned Pok Pok restaurant dynasty, and frequent poster of cat photos on Instagram (@pawkhrua). While drinking vinegars are often added to soda water, they're also a surprisingly refreshing layer of flavor in your cocktails. Flavors offered include Apple, Ginger, Honey, Pineapple, Pomegranate, Tamarind, Thai Basil, Chinese Celery, and Turmeric.

> High-Proof pick: The Thai Basil drinking vinegar is perfect for a host of different cocktails. I use it in gin cocktails like the Gin Rickey.

Portland Bitters Project

www.portlandbittersproject.com
Buy online or at retailers

Portland Bitters Project began in the fall of 2013 with the goal to create organic, therapeutic-grade, botanical bitters for cocktails and cooking. The process starts by immersing botanicals in organic spirits. After the blending process, raw cane sugar is added to the blend. Quintessentially Portland flavors include Woodland Bitters made with wild-crafted Douglas Fir, and Pitch Dark Cacao Bitters made with local Pitch Dark Madagascar cacao. The Aromatic Bitters and Super Spice Bitters are also a must-try.

> High-Proof pick: Woodland Bitters has an approachable, earthy and woodsy flavor that's versatile enough to use in both cocktails and cooking. Try sprinkling it on roasted root vegetables at your next meal for added brightness.

Shrub Works Co.

www.shrubworksco.com
Buy at retailers or bars

Nearly every time barman Aaron Bennett made a fresh batch of shrubs for Sidecar 11 on Mississippi Avenue, he noticed a trend: people wanted to buy his shrubs by the bottle. A few years later, after spending time as a brand ambassador for Big Bottom Distilling and working as a cocktail consultant, Aaron formed Shrub Works Co. The first shrubs, made from drop fruit from growers right outside of the city, went on sale at farmer's markets and bars around town. Shrub Works Co.'s current flavors include Orange/Rosemary, Green Tea/Bay Leaf/Peppercorn, Grapefruit/Raspberry, Cardamom/Lime/Apple, and Strawberry/Lavender.

> High-Proof pick: For the most versatile shrub, go for the Grapefruit/Raspberry. Not only is it refreshing in cocktails, but this one also goes nicely in salad dressings or marinades.

OTHER HOOCH MADE IN PORTLAND AND BEYOND (NO TASTING ROOM)

Portland is a sharing-centric, collaborative city. I've had strangers offer me a sip of their drink or a bit of their meal just for catching a glance. We're collaborative in more profound ways too. When it comes to owning a business in this town, those who get ahead collude with and support other businesses. That's how enthusiasts become distillers, and non-distillers release spirits. They either contract a distillery to help them produce a product, or they collaborate and use a larger distillery's very expensive equipment.

There are small-scale makers who have chosen to work with Portland-based distilleries to produce one-of-a-kind spirits, and a few companies produce spirits in-house but without a tasting room.

Dogwood Distilling

www.dogwooddistilling.com
Spirits: Branch Raw Honey Rye, DL Franklin Vodka,
Haint Absinthe, Union Gin

Dogwood Distilling aims to make fine mid-shelf liquors that display versatility while staying true to its microdistillery roots. Dogwood exceeds that goal better than anyone else out there. DL Franklin Vodka, the company's first product, is one of the best vodkas on the market for the price. It's got everything you want and expect from craft vodka: adaptability, mouthfeel, and accessibility. That tradition is carried through in the gin and absinthe too.

Dogwood's most recent project, Branch Raw Honey Rye, is a collaboration between Dogwood Distilling and Bee Local Honey. It's a clear spirit (101 proof; eighty percent malted barley and twenty percent malted rye) with a touch of dry sweetness from the honey. Located outside of Portland in Forest Grove, Dogwood Distilling has been producing spirits since 2010. All four of Dogwood Distilling's spirits are available from liquor stores around Oregon.

Double Circle Spirits

www.doublecirclespirits.com
Spirit: Columbia Plateau Vodka

Proprietor Jason Johnson, a native of The Dalles, Oregon, had always dreamed of using the wheat planted east of the Cascades in the late 1800s by his great, great grandfather. Then, in 2014 that dream and passion of starting a spirits company using that grain became a plan when he started Double

Circle Spirits. The plan came to fruition in 2015 with his first case of Double Circle Spirits Columbia Plateau Vodka distilled at New Deal Distilling. With a neutral aroma, it'll take until the sip to notice the difference that soft white wheat makes— it's mildly sweet and wheat forward. Johnson plans to continue growing the company with the production of gin, bourbon, and whiskey.

JVR Spirits

www.jvrspirits.com/krupnik
Spirits: Krupnik Spiced Honey Liqueur

Krupnik is a liqueur made from grain spirits and honey, popular in Lithuania and Poland. JVR's recipe is centuries old and has been made by Vince Radostitz's family for three generations. The branding is so hip and fresh that you'd never guess this could be the same recipe that a jada (the Polish word for grandpa) enjoyed. The Radostitz family starts with whole organic spices that are prepared the same day they make a batch. Next, organic citrus is added (cut and peeled by hand, of course). The secret ingredient is the honey sourced from the same family-owned business that Vince's father did business with forty years ago.

Why krupnik? After Vince's parents passed away, he and his nephew Casey found his father's krupnik kit while cleaning out the garage at his house. For fun, they decided to do a last batch. The smell was just as Vince remembered: herbal aromas mixed with the sweet smell of honey. The family recipe was soon resurrected.

Royalty Spirits
www.miruvodka.com
Spirit: Miru Vodka

In a primarily male dominated industry, Chaunci King, CEO of Royalty Spirits wanted to produce a product designed for women. After bartending for many years, King launched Royalty spirits in 2013 to produce Miru pear flavored vodka. According to Royalty Spirits, the name Miru originated from an old wives tale of a dominating Sea Goddess, which coincides with our plan to dominate the world of flavored vodkas. Royalty Spirits current product, Miru Vodka is a pear flavored vodka made from grain and pure spring water from the Pacific Cascades.

Troika Spirits
www.troikaspirits.com
Spirits: Kachka Horseradish Vodka

After getting their footing running Kachka, one of Portland's favorite Russian restaurants, owners Bonnie and Israel Morales decided to start dabbling in spirits. After all, so much of Russian fare does involve vodka.

In 2016, Bonnie and Israel founded Troika Spirits. The first spirit they released under the Troika label was the Kachka Horseradish Vodka. Each bottle of this infused vodka is hand-made using locally sourced whole horseradish root and a drop of honey. Troika Spirits currently produces and bottles its vodka at nearby New Deal Distillery. Prior to the distilling relationship with New Deal, Bonnie and Israel infused their horseradish vodka in-house at the restaurant. Those in search of authentic Old World vodka can find this infused vodka at New Deal Distillery.

PORTLAND-AREA DISTILLERY EVENTS & OUTINGS

Aside from smaller events at distilleries, such as launches and workshops, there are a few large-scale tasting events where a majority of the distillers come together to show off their portfolios.

Distillery Row's
The Cocktail Demystified

www.distilleryrowpdx.com/category/news/upcoming-events
$10 (advance) or $15 (at the door) for general admission

All eight of the Distillery Row distilleries meet to showcase over fifty products at this event. After sampling the spirits, take your bartending skills to the next level by attending the numerous cocktail-making presentations.

Feast Portland

www.feastportland.com
Prices vary: around $75 for Hands-On events;
$45 for Drink Tank events

National accolades and an experienced team led by Carrie Welch and Mike Thelin have made Feast Portland, now in its fifth year (2016), one of the most popular food and drink events in the country. Case in point: tickets for a John Gorham dinner (Gorham is the chef/owner of Portland's renowned Toro Bravo and Mediterranean Exploration Company sold out within seconds after being made available. Feast Portland is actually a series of different events. Smaller events and classes meet all over the city, but the larger events like the Main Events (the Sandwich Invitational, Brunch Village, Night Market, and others) and Dinner Series are perfect for those looking to mingle with the food and drink obsessed. The real deals for drinker lovers, though, are the Drink Tank and Hands-On events. For around $45 to $75, you can learn how to execute the perfect martini shake, meet famous bartenders, or soak in Tiki culture—all while drinking fabulous cocktails.

Great American Distillers Festival
www.distillersfestival.com
$20 (advance) or $25 (at the door) for general admission;
$100 for VIP tickets

This Portland tasting event features distillers from all over the country. Attendees are treated to dinners, product and packaging contests, new product sneak peeks, and cocktail matches. 2014 was the event's tenth year. Proceeds from the event benefit local charities, the Oregon Distillers Guild, and the Oregon Distillery Trail.

Oregon Distillers Festival at
McMenamins Edgefield
www.mcmenamins.com/Edgefield
$30 for general admission (includes fourteen tasting tokens)

McMenamins and the Oregon Distillers Guild throw a party on the Edgefield lawn in Troutdale, Oregon, an area that was once a 1911 county poor farm, and was later turned into a destination resort. Edgefield is also home to a McMenamins distillery that opened in 1998 and is housed in a dry shed that once stored vegetables grown at the Edgefield estate back when it was a farm. Sip over one hundred handcrafted spirits from more than twenty Oregon Distillers Guild members from around the state of Oregon.

Tiki Kon
www.tikikon.com
$63 for the Music & Symposium Pass; $179 for the Full Weekend Pass; $299 for the VIP Weekend Pass

There are cocktail buffs—and then there are Tiki fans. Tiki cocktails are having a bit of a moment right now. The Tiki fans, however, have been celebrating Tiki culture since 2003. Taking place over the summer in Portland, Tiki Kon, the annual symposium of all things Polynesian, rounds out with a home bar tour. Tiki Kon started as a bar crawl between friends' basements and has since turned into full-blown "Polynesian-Pop Extravaganza" celebrating Tiki bars and cocktails, as well as the art, music, and fashion it inspires.

TOAST: The Original Artisan Spirits Tasting
Presented by the Oregon Distillers Guild
www.oregondistillerytrail.com/general-information
$45 for general admission; $60 for VIP tickets; $15 for DD tickets

For over six years, attendees have experienced "120 spirits from across the Pacific Northwest, the country, and the globe," which ends up being nearly forty distillers under one roof. In recent years, local Portland chefs have prepared small bites here too.

WhiskeyTown USA
www.whiskeytownusa.com
$50 for general admission (includes eight tasting tokens)

On any given year, when WhiskeyTown rolls into Portland, there are over two hundred types of whiskey available to sample, including Oregon-made varieties. This celebration of whiskey includes educational events, cocktail competitions, music performances, food, and much, much more.

HANGOVER CURES
(or, how to deal with the unpleasant symptoms of excessive alcohol)

I have the highest hopes that you sip and savor the spirits at the distilleries you visit, and treat your day as more of an exploration than a Booze Cruise; however, I realize that some booze often leads to more booze, which can result in a hangover.

If you're legally old enough to drink, you've probably already experienced at least one memorable hangover and likely have your own remedies, but there's always room for new strategies and tips, and always room for more acceptance and less shame and sheepish excuses.

WHAT THE EXPERTS SAY

Now that you've developed an interest in distilling, you'll need to refine your strategy for dealing with hangovers. I've had a lot of hangovers over the years.

Developing a deeper interest in spirits doesn't necessarily mean we're more reckless, but it doesn't mean we're immune. When a hangover does creep in, we have to be prepared. In the past, you may have suffered through the day, crying into a box of Popeye's Biscuits. Lucky for us all, Portland has a lot of options for hair of the dog remedies, and many bartenders and drink purveyors with advice to help you cope, whether it's by sliding a Bloody Mary across the bar at you, or these wise words I've collected:

> "My go-to cure to a hangover is a cocktail called the Corpse Grinder. It's a play on a Corpse Reviver with a few ingredients swapped out. Mine has gin, Combier, Cocchi Americano, grapefruit juice, and absinthe. It reminds you of all the best parts of the

night before without the end-of-the-night haze."

—*Jon Lewis*
Bar Manager at Rue

"Either Topo Chico, a Mexican mineral water that is life-in-a-bottle, or club soda of some kind helps. Peppermint oil on my temples for my headache and sipping ice cold sweet mint tea also works. But my secret is actually grocery store sushi. I have a huge craving for grocery store sushi when I'm hungover. I usually get a mixed avocado and cucumber and a tuna; those are the best!"

—*Mindy Kucan*
Bartender and Tiki Drink Expert at Hale Pele

"I have a couple of tricks for hangovers. One was made popular when I was down in New Orleans. Cocktail tour guides would recommend this cure to some of their ailing guests:

'Shake these ingredients and serve over ice with either soda water or ginger beer: 1 ounce of Angostura Bitters, 1 ounce fresh lemon juice, and 1 ounce honey syrup (2 parts honey to one part hot water, stir) or ginger syrup (I like El Guapo Bitters Ginger Syrup if you don't want to make your own).'

My mom's old standby was a cheeseburger, some fries, and a soda. I, on the other hand, turn toward a good burrito. For a cure-all beverage, Pedialyte (my favorite flavor is grape) and coconut water are both outstanding. I keep Pedialyte popsicles in my freezer and love those with saltine crackers and some Advil. Sex is another good one. The chemicals your body releases are a great way to counteract the misery of a hangover."

—Becca June
Bartender at Lafitte's at The Waiting Room,
and Secretary of the Oregon Bartender's Guild

"I've experimented with hair of the dog, but it usually makes me feel worse. There are some liqueurs with gentian root proven to help with nausea. It doesn't take much, maybe ¾ ounce of Aveze Gentiane Liqueur. Be sure to add soda too.

Did I mention bacon? For lunch, I stick to comfort foods and go for a cheeseburger with a milkshake.

Another pro tip: when you're out on the town drinking, try to remember to drink plenty of water in between drinks. Before you turn in, drink another glass of water along with a B vitamin. This is probably the best strategy I know for prevention."

—*Tommy Klus, Barman at La Moule*

"As much sleep as possible, about four Ibuprofen, a ton of water, sex, a run at the gym for thirty minutes, and then some real good ramen and a Budweiser—works every time."

—*Joel Westrom, bartender at Rum Club*

"If we're talking an epic, can-barely-crawl-out-of-bed hangover, then I'll probably just make my way across the street to Burgerville for a chocolate shake, and then take it easy until I'm feeling up for going out again. Fortunately, those hangovers are pretty rare. More typically, nothing beats a good

spicy noodle soup. My go-to choice is the Mhoo
, Tom Yum at Mee Sen Thai Eatery on Mississippi
Avenue."

—*Jacob Grier, Author of Cocktails on Tap: The Art of Mixing*
Spirits and Beer, occasional Bartender at Multnomah
Whiskey Library, and Founder of Aquavit Week

"For me, it's all about jumping back on the horse and
getting to it. I start with a hot shower followed by an
Emergen-C in bubbly water paired with vitamins.
Then I roll myself over to Stanich's Hamburgers and
dive into a pint of cheap beer and a double cheeseburger. And, just like that, I'm back in the saddle."

—*Jesse Card, previously General Manager at Bit House*
Saloon; has an extensive background in
hangover acquisitions

FIVE STEPS TO DEALING
WITH A HANGOVER

- Never battle a hangover
  alone.

- Utilize hair of the dog
  earlier rather than later.

- Don't forget that it's
  your fault.

- Stop whining and eat
  more.

- Promise to never drink
  that much again.

ABV (alcohol by volume)
ABV is the worldwide standard measurement of alcohol (pure ethanol) contained in a given volume of an alcoholic beverage. See also proof.

Aquavit
A Scandinavian spirit made with botanicals and distilled from grain. The main flavor is caraway seed, which is balanced with other flavors, such as anise, citrus, coriander, cumin, dill, fennel, juniper, or star anise.

Baijiu (BYE-joe)
Baijiu is an ancient clear spirit that originated in China made from one or more of these ingredients: sorghum, wheat, rice, sticky rice, and/or corn.

Bitters
Bitters are a liquid extraction of herbs, seeds, bark, fruit or other plants. Add a dash or three of bitters to your cocktail for complex flavors.

Bourbon
Bourbon is simply a whiskey. It's made from a grain mixture that has to be at least fifty-one percent corn and aged in new, charred oak barrels.

Brandy
A strong spirit distilled from wine or fermented fruit juice.

Caipirinha
Brazil's national cocktail made with cachaça (sugarcane liquor), sugar, and lime.

Craft spirit

To be defined as craft, a spirit has to be made by an independently owned distillery that has a maximum annual production of only fifty-two thousand cases. The spirit also has to be distilled and bottled on-site.

Column Still (Reflux Still)

A column still is a type of still commonly used to produce American whiskey and vodka. These stills work like a bunch of single pot stills arranged in a long vertical tube. Plates fill the vertical tube so that the rising vapor can condense in the higher and cooler levels of the column or tube.

Distillation

The magical process that gives us our beloved booze. Specifically, it's the separation of a liquid by selective evaporation and condensation.

Distillery Row

Commonly refers to the collective of distilleries (currently eight) located in Southeast Portland, but it also refers to the general marketing initiative (www.distilleryrowpdx.com) celebrating distilling and drinking culture in Portland.

Eau de Vie

This generally colorless and super dry brandy is made from fermenting fruit rather than distilling that fermented fruit into a fruit mash.

Gin

Gin is distilled from grains and can vary in flavor depending on the botanical ingredients added. Gin's strong piney flavor comes from juniper berries.

Grappa

Grappa is a pomace brandy distilled from the skins, pulp, and seeds that are left over from the winemaking process, generally after the grapes have been pressed.

Hair of the Dog
A colloquial expression that refers to a typical remedy for hangovers. It's usually a small or weak alcoholic beverage intended to wean drinkers off slowly.

Heads
In the distillation process, the "head" is the first thing off of the still. Only brave distillers should taste the spirit at this point.

Hearts
In the distillation process, the "heart" of the spirit is the best part of distillate. If it's an un-aged product, this is what will be eventually bottled. When you drink, you are drinking the heart of the run.

IBU (International Bitterness Units)
IBU is the measure of a beer's bitterness, generally an indication of the concentration or type of hops used during the brewing process. The addition of malt can affect the flavor, however, and can make a beer with a higher IBU taste less bitter than a beer with a lower IBU.

Kombucha
A fermented tea using bacteria and yeast. The outcome is a lightly effervescent tea with supposed health benefits.

Krupnik
A liqueur made from grain spirits and honey, popular in Lithuania and Poland. One Portland purveyor, JVR Spirits, is ensuring Portland has locally produced krupnik.

Liqueur
A liqueur is an alcoholic beverage flavored with fruit, herbs, spices, or flowers, with sugar or sweetener added. Don't

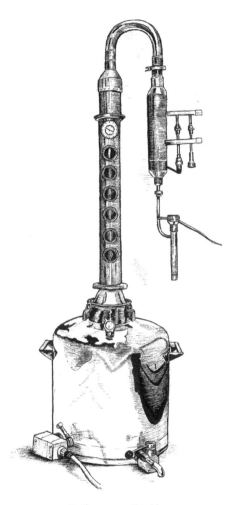

Column Still

underestimate the ABV; you can still get drunk drinking liqueurs.

Mash

In the distillation process, the mash is the resulting mixture from combining and heating grains like corn, malted barely, sorghum, rye, or wheat with water.

Mezcal

A spirit made from the heart of the maguey plant (a type of agave) grown in parts of Mexico, primarily the Oaxaca region. This aged spirit is smoky and earthy in taste.

NW Distiller's District

The collection of distilleries in Northwest Portland composed of Clear Creek Distillery, Bull Run Distilling Company, Martin Ryan Distilling Company (Aria Gin).

Oregon Liquor Control Commission (OLCC)

The OLCC controls distribution, sales, and consumption of alcohol in the state of Oregon. It also buys a lot of liquor from Portland distillers to stock in its own liquor stores, and it pays on time. This means that distillers tend not to mind the OLCC that much.

Pot still

A type of still commonly used to make whiskey or brandy. The heat in the process is applied to the pot containing the mash.

Proof

Proof is a measure of the amount of alcohol in a spirit. A spirit's proof can be found by multiplying the percentage of alcohol (ABV) by two. For example, a spirit with 50 ABV is 100 proof. See also ABV.

Rum

Primarily made from a sugarcane by-product like molasses.

Rum ranges from silver, or white rum, to amber, or dark rum, depending on whether it's been aged or not, or if it was made from molasses.

Rye Whiskey
Whiskey made from a mash that's made up of at least fifty-one percent rye.

Sorghum
Sorghum is a grassy plant that ferments quickly. It's a prominent grain in certain styles of baijiu.

Still
One of the most important pieces of equipment used in the distillation process, the still is used to heat and selectively boil the liquid mash, as well as to cool and condense the resulting vapor into the distillate.

Tails
In the distillation process, the "tail" is the last bit of spirit product that comes out of the still. It isn't great for drinking but can be combined with the "head" for redistillation in some cases.

Tequila
A spirit distilled from blue agave grown in Jalisco, Mexico and some surrounding areas—and that shot you had one too many of in college.

Whiskey, or Whisky
Made from fermented grain mash, whiskey is basically beer (without the hops) before it's been distilled. The distillate is then aged in charred oak barrels, typically for ten to twenty years for really top-shelf productions, though whiskey can develop complex flavors at three to five years. The Irish spell it "whiskey," while the Scots use "whisky."

Vermouth

Think of vermouth as the concoction your Aunt Dorothy would mix up by adding spirits to her wine. Vermouth is basically a fortified wine used in cocktails or for sipping, meaning the ABV is raised with the addition of wine.

Vodka

Made up of water and ethanol, vodka is made from fermented grains or potatoes. Often, vodka is the first spirit a distillery makes because it's cheaper than gin or whiskey and doesn't require any aging time.

NOTES